Dating Someone with Complex PTSD

A Guide to the Early Stages of Loving a Trauma Survivor

Mortimer Thaddeus Ashbourne

This book is intended for general informational and educational purposes only. It is not a substitute for professional medical, psychological, or psychiatric advice, diagnosis, or treatment. The content provided does not create a therapeutic or clinical relationship between the author and the reader.

No guarantee of specific outcomes or results is made or implied. Every individual and every relationship is different, and the information in this book should be applied with personal judgment and professional guidance where appropriate. Readers are encouraged to consult qualified mental health professionals for individualized support.

All names, characters, and scenarios presented in this book are composites drawn from common clinical presentations and educational examples. They do not represent any specific individual, living or deceased. Any resemblance to actual persons, events, or situations is coincidental. These examples are used solely for illustrative and educational purposes and are not intended to harm, misrepresent, or identify any person or entity.

The author and copyright holder disclaim any liability for actions taken or not taken based on the contents of this book.

First Edition:

ISBN: 9781764576383

Table of Contents

Preface

Every book about loving someone with PTSD assumes you have already decided to stay. This one starts earlier.

It starts in the parking lot after a date that ended abruptly and without explanation. It starts at two in the morning, when you are reading forums and articles and finding advice written for people ten years into a marriage, not ten weeks into something new. It starts with a question that sounds simple but carries enormous weight: What is happening, and what should I do about it?

If you have already searched for help, you have probably found the same advice repeated in different words. Be patient. Be understanding. Educate yourself. The advice is not wrong. It is incomplete. It does not account for the fact that you are at the beginning of something, not the middle. It does not acknowledge that you have no established trust to draw on, no shared history to anchor you, and no commitment binding you to what comes next. You are choosing, right now, in real time, how much of yourself to invest in a relationship whose patterns you cannot yet read.

That gap between the advice available and the situation you are actually in is the reason this book was written.

Complex Post-Traumatic Stress Disorder is a condition that develops from repeated relational harm, most commonly during childhood. Unlike standard PTSD, which typically follows a single event, Complex PTSD reshapes how a person relates to others, how they see themselves, and how their body manages closeness and stress. These effects do not wait for a convenient moment to appear. They surface in the first weeks and months of a new relationship, often before either partner has language for what is happening.

The person you are dating may not carry a formal diagnosis. They may not know the term Complex PTSD. They may describe their struggles as anxiety, depression, attachment issues, or simply the way they have always been. But the patterns are recognizable once you know what to look for: the sudden withdrawal after closeness, the emotional reactions that seem disconnected from the present moment, the difficulty with trust that feels personal even when it is not.

This book will teach you those patterns. It will explain what your partner's nervous system is doing during the moments that confuse you most. It will give you practical tools, script banks, and frameworks you can use immediately, not after years of study. And it will do something that few books in this space are willing to do: it will ask you to examine your own role in the dynamic, to consider what your history brings to the table, and to make a clear-eyed decision about what this relationship is worth to you.

What this book will not do is tell you that love alone is enough, that patience will solve everything, or that your only job is to endure. Your experience matters. Your needs are real. And the decision about what comes next belongs to you.

The chapters ahead are organized around the sequence of challenges that most early-stage partners encounter: the initial confusion, the nervous system patterns behind it, the push-pull cycle, the moments when trauma surfaces without warning, the conversation about the past, the complexities of physical intimacy, the caretaker trap, the mirror of your own history, the hardest question of all, and, finally, a realistic picture of what a good outcome looks like when both people show up.

Every story in this book is a composite, drawn from common clinical presentations and educational examples. No individual is represented. The scenarios are designed to help you recognize patterns, not to diagnose anyone, including yourself.

You picked up this book because something in your relationship does not make sense. By the time you finish it, it will.

Chapter 1 You're Not Losing Your Mind— And Neither Are They

Margot met Felix at a friend's dinner party on a Friday night in October. He was funny, attentive, and disarmingly honest about his love of bad movies and good coffee. They talked for three hours. He walked her to her car and asked if she wanted to get dinner the following week. She said yes before he finished the sentence.

The first three dates were, by Margot's own account, the best she had ever been on. Felix asked questions and actually listened to the answers. He remembered details. He showed up on time, made her laugh, and kissed her goodnight in a way that felt both confident and gentle. Margot told her best friend she thought she had finally found someone real.

On the fourth date, something shifted. They were sitting at a restaurant she had chosen, a place with warm lighting and good wine, when Felix went quiet. Not thoughtful-quiet. Absent-quiet. His face changed in a way Margot could not describe except to say the person sitting across from her suddenly felt like someone she had never met. She asked if everything was okay. He said he was fine. He smiled, but the smile did not reach his eyes. He excused himself to go to the restroom and was gone for twelve minutes.

When he came back, he changed the subject to something light. They finished dinner. He drove her home and kissed her on the cheek. And then she did not hear from him for five days.

During those five days, Margot replayed every moment of the evening. She checked her phone forty times. She drafted and deleted eight text messages. She asked herself what she had done wrong. She asked herself if the restaurant had been a bad choice. She asked herself if she had said something offensive without realizing it. She asked herself if Felix was seeing someone else. She searched the internet for "why did he go quiet on our date." She found nothing that made sense.

When Felix finally texted, he was warm, apologetic in a vague way, and eager to see her again. The next date was wonderful. The one after that ended with him leaving abruptly because of a sudden headache. Then three more days of silence.

Margot did not know it yet, but she was falling in love with a man who has Complex PTSD. And everything that was confusing her had a name, a cause, and a pattern she could learn to read.

This chapter is the one that should have been waiting for you the moment you started searching. The confusion you are feeling is not a sign that something is wrong with your instincts. It is the natural response of a reasonable person encountering a set of behaviors that make no sense without the right framework. That framework is what this book provides. It begins here, with the single most important thing you need to understand: what you are seeing in your new partner has a clinical name, a known set of patterns, and a logic that, once you learn it, will change every conversation you have about this relationship going forward.

The Confusion Is the First Clue

If you picked up this book, something happened that left a mark on you,something you still can't quite explain. Maybe it was the vanishing act after a night that felt almost perfect, leaving you replaying every moment, searching for the point where it all went wrong. Maybe it was the way their warmth turned to distance in an instant, like a door quietly closing in your face. Or maybe it was a reaction so sharp, so disproportionate, that it shook you—left you sitting alone afterward, heart heavy, wondering if you had somehow imagined the connection, the closeness, the entire experience.

You didn't imagine it.

The early stages of dating someone with Complex PTSD produce a specific kind of confusion that is unlike anything else in relationships. It is not the ordinary uncertainty of new dating, the "does he like me" question, or the slow realization that you want different things. This is different. This is the feeling of watching someone switch channels in front of you, moving from fully present to fully gone in a span of minutes, with no warning and no clear cause.

Clara described it this way. "It was like dating two different people. On Monday, he would text me good morning and we would talk for an hour and I felt like the most important person in the world. By Wednesday, I would get one-word answers. By Friday, nothing. Then Sunday, flowers and a long voice message telling me how much he missed me."

Clara was not dating someone who was playing games. She was dating someone whose nervous system was cycling between states of perceived safety and perceived danger, and she had no way of knowing that because nobody had ever explained it to her.

Here is what makes early dating with a Complex PTSD survivor uniquely difficult compared to other relational challenges. In most relationships, problems surface slowly. Incompatibility reveals itself over months. Communication differences emerge gradually. With Complex PTSD, the difficulty can appear without warning on a Tuesday night at a perfectly nice restaurant, and then disappear completely by Thursday morning, leaving you to wonder if anything happened at all.

The confusion is not a side effect. It is the central experience. And the fact that you feel it so strongly is actually useful information. It tells you that the person you are dating is carrying something that affects how they connect, and that what you are reading as rejection, inconsistency, or disinterest is almost certainly something else entirely.

Complex PTSD Has a Name and a Logic

Post-Traumatic Stress Disorder, as most people understand it, develops after a single overwhelming event. A car accident. A violent assault. A combat experience. A natural disaster. The brain records the event as an ongoing threat, and the person relives it through flashbacks, nightmares, hypervigilance, and avoidance of anything connected to the original event.

Complex PTSD is something different. It develops not from one terrible moment, but from repeated exposure to harm over an extended period, usually during childhood, and usually at the hands of someone who was supposed to provide safety. A parent who was unpredictable. A caregiver who was neglectful, abusive, or emotionally volatile. A home environment where the child could not escape, could not predict what would happen next, and could not rely on the adults around them for protection (Herman, 1992).

The distinction matters enormously for dating. A person with standard PTSD after a car accident may flinch at the sound of screeching tires. Their partner can learn that specific response and adjust for it. It is a focused sensitivity with identifiable cues.

A person with Complex PTSD carries something broader and harder to map. Because the original wounds happened inside relationships, inside the very bonds that were supposed to be safe, closeness itself can become the alarm. Love can feel like danger. Being wanted can feel like being trapped. The warmth of a new partner can set off the same nervous system responses that once protected a child from an unpredictable parent.

This is the piece that most people miss, and that most books about PTSD fail to address directly. Your partner's reactions are not about the surface of what is happening between you. They are about a much older conversation, one that started long before they met you, between their body and the idea of what it means to need someone.

Judith Herman, the psychiatrist who first described Complex PTSD in her landmark 1992 work, identified symptoms beyond standard PTSD that cluster into three areas: difficulties regulating emotions, a persistently negative sense of self, and problems in relationships (Herman, 1992). The World Health Organization formally recognized Complex PTSD as a distinct diagnosis in the ICD-11, confirming what clinicians had observed for decades: repeated relational harm creates a different kind of wound than a single event (World Health Organization, 2019). More recent research has shown that Complex PTSD and standard PTSD are indeed separable conditions with distinct symptom profiles, not simply variations of the same disorder (Cloitre et al., 2013).

For you, the new partner, here is what that means in practical terms. Standard PTSD has more predictable contours. Complex PTSD is woven into the fabric of how your partner relates to other people, how they see themselves, and how they manage their own emotional life. All three of those dimensions will show up in your dating relationship, often before either of you has language for what is happening. Understanding this distinction is the difference between feeling lost and having a map.

The two conditions share several features: intrusive memories, avoidance of reminders, heightened startle responses, and difficulty sleeping. But Complex PTSD adds three layers that directly affect how your partner functions in a romantic relationship. First, their emotional responses may swing rapidly and intensely in ways that seem disconnected from the present moment. Second, they may carry a deeply held belief that they are defective, unlovable, or fundamentally broken. Third, they may find close relationships both desperately needed and deeply threatening, sometimes within the same hour. These three additional layers are what make Complex PTSD a relationship condition in a way that standard PTSD is not, and they are what brought you to this book.

Three Patterns That Change Everything

The clinical literature identifies several symptom clusters in Complex PTSD, but for someone in the early weeks or months of a new relationship, three patterns tend to surface first and cause the most confusion.

The first is the one you probably noticed earliest. Your partner reacts to something, a comment, a tone, a small change in plans, with an intensity that does not match the situation. Gabriel saw this on his fifth date with Paloma. They had spent a Saturday afternoon at a farmer's market, laughing and trying samples, and he made an offhand joke about her being "a little too organized" when she rearranged the groceries in his bag. Paloma stopped talking. Her face went flat. She spent the rest of the drive home looking out the window, and when he walked her to her door, she thanked him formally, like he was a stranger who had given her a ride.

Gabriel spent that night convinced he had been insensitive. He was ready to apologize, but he genuinely did not know for what. What he did not know was that Paloma's mother had spent years criticizing her for small domestic failures, and that any comment about how she organized or arranged things could flood her body with shame so old and so automatic that Paloma herself could not always connect it to its source. In clinical terms, Paloma experienced what therapist Pete Walker calls an **emotional flashback**, a sudden overwhelming wave of the feelings from a past traumatic experience without a clear visual memory attached (Walker, 2013). She did not see her mother's face. She did not consciously think about her childhood. She simply felt, in her whole body, the familiar sense of being inadequate and exposed.

This is emotional dysregulation as it appears in Complex PTSD, and it looks nothing like the pop-culture image of someone overreacting. From the outside, it can look like silent withdrawal, sudden coldness, or an abrupt shutdown. From the inside, your partner may be drowning in feelings they cannot name, coming from a place they cannot locate, with an intensity that bewilders them just as much as it bewilders you.

The second pattern involves trust, and it will feel personal even though it is not. Your partner may ask you the same reassuring question multiple times. They may interpret a delayed text response as evidence of rejection. They may pull back after a moment of closeness, as if the closeness itself was too much. They may tell you something personal and then immediately regret it, becoming distant or defensive for days afterward.

Zoe noticed this early on with Elio. After their third date, Elio told her about his childhood in a way that was brief and carefully worded. The next morning, he canceled their plans for the weekend. When Zoe asked why, he said he was busy. She later learned that Elio had panicked after sharing personal information, convinced that Zoe would think less of him or, worse, use what he had told her as a weapon later. His withdrawal was not about Zoe. It was about every person before Zoe who had received a piece of his story and had handled it carelessly.

For people with Complex PTSD, trust is not a switch that flips once and stays on. It is an ongoing negotiation between the present, where you are showing up consistently, and the past, where everyone who showed up consistently eventually caused pain. The result is a pattern that can feel maddening from the outside: your partner wants closeness, moves toward it, achieves it, and then retreats as if burned. They are not playing a game. They are following an internal logic that says closeness and pain are the same thing, because for a very long time, they were.

The third early pattern is subtler but just as important. People with Complex PTSD often carry a profoundly distorted sense of themselves. They may believe they are fundamentally flawed, unworthy of genuine love, or destined to ruin anything good. This belief is not a mood that passes. It is a deeply held conviction, installed by years of being treated as though they were too much, not enough, or the cause of the problems around them.

In early dating, this shows up in surprising ways. Your partner may struggle to receive compliments. They may deflect praise with humor or dismiss it entirely. They may sabotage moments of genuine connection because, at some level, they do not believe they deserve them. Or they may overperform, reading your desires and reflecting them back so perfectly that you feel like you have met the ideal partner, only to discover weeks or months later that the person you fell for was a carefully constructed version designed to be whatever you wanted.

This last pattern, the over-accommodation and the shape-shifting, is sometimes the hardest to recognize because it does not look like a problem. It looks like compatibility. It looks like someone who shares all your interests, agrees with all your opinions, and wants exactly what you want. But underneath that performance is a person who learned, very young, that the only way to stay safe in a relationship was to become what the other person needed. Clinicians call this the fawn response, a term coined by Pete Walker, and it is one of the most important dynamics to understand in early dating (Walker, 2013). We will return to it in the next chapter, because when fawning is the first thing you encounter in a new relationship, everything that follows will make more sense once you see it clearly.

Think about the last moment in this relationship that left you genuinely confused. Ask yourself one question: Was the reaction you saw about what was happening between you right then, or could it have been about something much older? You do not need to answer the question yet. You just need to start asking it. That shift, from "what did I do wrong?" to "what might this be connected to?", is the beginning of a new way of seeing everything that happens between you.

They May Not Have the Words for It Yet

Here is something that may surprise you. Your partner may not know they have Complex PTSD. The condition was formally recognized by the World Health Organization only in 2019, and it still does not appear as a separate diagnosis in the American Psychiatric Association's DSM-5-TR. Many clinicians, particularly those not specializing in trauma, may not assess for it specifically.

Noemi dated Julian for four months before a mutual friend, a social worker, gently mentioned the term. Julian had been in therapy for years for what had been described as anxiety and depression. He had tried medication for both. He had been told he had an avoidant attachment style. All of these descriptions were partially accurate, but none of them captured the full picture: the emotional flashbacks, the difficulty managing his reactions to perceived criticism, the deep belief that he was fundamentally broken, and the way closeness with Noemi made him feel simultaneously alive and terrified.

When Noemi read about Complex PTSD, she told Julian it was the first description that had ever made complete sense of what she was observing. Julian read the same material and wept. He later told her it was the first time in his life that he felt recognized by a clinical description.

Many survivors of childhood trauma carry their symptoms without a name for them. They know they struggle in relationships. They know their reactions can be disproportionate. They know something is off, but they have spent their lives being told they are too sensitive, too intense, too difficult, or too broken in ways that cannot be fixed. Some have been given other diagnoses that capture part of the picture but not all of it. Some have never sought professional help. Some are actively in treatment but have not yet reached the layer of work where Complex PTSD becomes visible.

This means you cannot expect your partner to hand you a diagnosis and a roadmap. You may be the first person to name what you are observing, and you need to do that with extraordinary care. This book will help you find that language. But for now, the most important thing to understand is this: their lack of a label does not mean the pattern is not real, and your confusion is not a sign that you are reading too much into things. You are reading the situation accurately. You just need the right lens.

Know What This Book Can and Cannot Do

This book is for the person who is in the early stages of dating someone with Complex PTSD, or who suspects that is what they are dealing with, and who wants to understand what is happening before deciding what comes next. It is written for you, the partner, because your experience matters too, and because the decisions you make in these early months will shape everything that follows.

This book is not a substitute for professional mental health treatment, for your partner or for you. It is not a program that will cure Complex PTSD. It does not ask you to become your partner's therapist, rescuer, or emotional shock absorber.

And it is not a manual for enduring abuse.

That last point needs to be stated clearly. Complex PTSD can explain certain behaviors: the withdrawal, the emotional intensity, the difficulty with trust. It does not excuse cruelty, contempt, intimidation, or violence. If you are in a relationship where you feel consistently unsafe, controlled, or degraded, the explanation for that behavior matters far less than your own safety. This book will address the distinction between trauma responses and abusive behavior directly in Chapter 9, because that line is one of the most important things you will ever learn to draw.

For the reader who is confused, scared, in love, and trying to figure out what is happening in their new relationship: you are in the right place. The chapters ahead will give you a working understanding of what your partner's nervous system is doing, what the common relational patterns look like and why they happen, how to offer support without losing yourself, and how to decide if this relationship is right for you.

Before you turn the page, take five minutes with a pen and paper. Write down the three specific moments that confused you most in this relationship so far. Do not analyze them yet. Do not try to explain them. Just describe what happened, as specifically as you can: the date, the setting, what was said, what shifted, and what you felt afterward. You will return to this list throughout the book, and each chapter will help you read one more layer of these moments. For now, naming them is enough.

What brought you here was confusion. What you will leave with is clarity.

Key Takeaways

What you are experiencing in your new relationship has a clinical name: Complex PTSD. It develops from repeated relational harm, most often during childhood, and it shapes how your partner connects with other people, how they perceive themselves, and how they manage their own emotional states.

Three patterns tend to appear first in early dating. Emotional reactions that do not match the present moment. Trust that moves in unpredictable cycles of closeness and retreat. And a distorted self-image that can range from harsh self-criticism to chameleon-like over-accommodation designed to keep you happy at their own expense.

Your partner may not have been diagnosed. They may not have language for what is happening inside them. They may be as confused by their own behavior as you are.

This book is a guide for the early stages of your relationship, not a treatment plan, not a substitute for professional support, and not an instruction to endure mistreatment in the name of compassion. The confusion that brought you here is real. The patterns you are seeing have a logic. And each chapter ahead will replace a piece of that confusion with practical understanding you can use right now.

Chapter 2 The Nervous System Is Running the Show

Hugo had been dating Lucia for six weeks when it happened for the first time at his apartment. They were on his couch watching a film, her feet tucked under his leg, a bowl of popcorn between them. Everything was easy. She was laughing at the dialogue and making fun of the actors. Then a scene shifted. A man on screen raised his voice at a woman in a kitchen, and Lucia went still.

Hugo did not notice at first. The scene was brief, maybe forty seconds, and the film moved on. But when he glanced over, Lucia's face had changed. Her eyes were open but unfocused. Her body was rigid against the cushions. He said her name. She did not respond. He said it again, touched her shoulder, and she flinched so hard the popcorn spilled across the floor.

"Sorry," she said, her voice thin and far away. "I think I need to go."

She left within three minutes. She was polite but mechanical, like someone following an evacuation procedure. Hugo stood at his door watching her walk to her car and could not make sense of a single thing that had just happened. Ten minutes earlier, they had been laughing. Now she was driving away from him without explanation, and something in her eyes had looked like the fear of a person in actual danger.

He texted her that night. She responded the next morning with a short message saying she was sorry she had been "weird" and could they please not talk about it. Hugo agreed, because he did not know what else to do. But the question followed him for days: What happened on that couch? And why did it feel like Lucia left the room long before she walked out the door?

What Hugo witnessed was not a mood swing, a personality flaw, or a sign that Lucia was losing interest. It was a nervous system response, fast, involuntary, and ancient in its origins. And until he understood what was driving that response, every confusing moment in their relationship would remain exactly that: confusing. This chapter gives you the framework Hugo needed. It explains what your partner's nervous system is doing during the moments that baffle you most, and why understanding the body's role changes everything about how you respond.

Your Partner Has Two Operating Systems

The human nervous system has two primary modes, and your partner's body shifts between them far more rapidly and dramatically than most people's. The first mode is the sympathetic nervous system, which prepares the body for action. When the sympathetic system activates, heart rate increases, muscles tense, breathing becomes shallow, and the body floods with stress hormones designed to fuel a response. This is the system behind what most people know as the fight-or-flight response.

The second mode involves the parasympathetic nervous system, specifically a branch of it that neuroscientist Stephen Porges calls the dorsal vagal complex (Porges, 2011). When this system takes over, the body does not speed up. It shuts down. Heart rate drops. Energy collapses. The person may feel numb, foggy, disconnected from their own body, or suddenly exhausted in a way that has nothing to do with sleep. This is the freeze response, and it is what Hugo saw on his couch that night. Lucia did not choose to leave. Her body decided for her.

In a person without a trauma history, these two systems activate in response to genuine threats and return to baseline relatively quickly. In a person with Complex PTSD, the systems are calibrated differently. Years of living in an unsafe environment trained the nervous system to detect danger everywhere, respond faster, respond harder, and stay activated longer. As we discussed in Chapter 1, Complex PTSD develops from repeated relational harm, usually in childhood. The nervous system learned its lessons during that time, and it has not received the update that the danger is over.

For you, the new partner, this means something both simple and profound. Many of the behaviors that confuse you are not decisions your partner is making. They are responses their body is producing. And the body moves faster than thought. By the time your partner can think about what is happening, their nervous system has already decided what to do about it.

Four Survival Responses and How They Appear on a Date

Therapist Pete Walker identified four primary survival responses that people with Complex PTSD cycle through, often without conscious awareness: fight, flight, freeze, and fawn (Walker, 2013). Each one looks different on a date than it does in a textbook, and recognizing them in real time is one of the most useful skills you can develop in this relationship.

The fight response does not always look like anger. Sometimes it shows up as sudden sharpness, a critical comment that seems to come from nowhere, or a defensive reaction to something harmless. Sebastian noticed this on a Saturday morning when he offered to make breakfast for Coralie. She had stayed over for the first time, and he was trying to be thoughtful. When he asked how she liked her eggs, she snapped, "I can make my own food.

I'm not helpless." The shift lasted about thirty seconds. Then Coralie softened, apologized, and changed the subject. Sebastian spent the rest of the morning wondering what he had done wrong. The answer was nothing. Coralie's nervous system had read a moment of being cared for as a moment of being controlled, because in her childhood home, offers of help had always come with strings attached.

The flight response in early dating rarely looks like someone running out of a room. It looks like canceling plans at the last minute. It looks like suddenly being "really busy with work" after a week of constant contact. It looks like physically leaving a conversation that was getting too close to something real. Martin saw this pattern with Eloise after their first month of dating. Every time they had a particularly good weekend together, Eloise would become unreachable for two or three days. She was not seeing other people. She was not angry. She was managing a nervous system that had learned long ago that good things are followed by bad things, and the only way to prepare for the bad thing is to create distance before it arrives.

The freeze response is what Hugo saw with Lucia. It is the body's last resort, the response that activates when fight and flight are not available or have not worked. A person in freeze may go blank in the middle of a conversation. They may stare at you without seeing you. They may become very still and very quiet, and when they come back, they may not remember clearly what happened. This response is closely linked to dissociation, a process in which the mind temporarily disconnects from the present moment as a form of protection (Van der Kolk, 2014). In early dating, freeze can happen during moments of physical closeness, during emotionally charged conversations, or, as Hugo learned, during something as ordinary as a movie scene that the body recognized even when the mind did not.

The fawn response is the one that deserves the most attention in the context of new relationships, because it is the hardest to spot and the most likely to mislead you. A person in fawn mode does not withdraw or lash out. They become excessively agreeable. They mirror your interests, your opinions, and your desires with uncanny accuracy. They suppress their own needs entirely and focus all their energy on making you happy. As we discussed in Chapter 1, this can look like the perfect partner. It is not. It is a survival strategy, developed in childhood to appease an unpredictable or dangerous caregiver, and it will eventually collapse under the weight of the real person's real needs.

Valeria saw this in herself during her first relationship after years of therapy. She recognized, three months in, that she had been agreeing with everything Oscar said, eating food she did not like because he chose the restaurants, and pretending to love hiking because he was passionate about it. She had not done any of this consciously. Her nervous system had simply run the old program: figure out what they want and become it. The moment she noticed it, she felt a wave of grief, because she realized she had no idea what she actually wanted from the relationship. She had been too busy performing safety to find out.

Take a moment to think about what you have observed in your partner during the moments that confused you most. Did they become sharp or critical without apparent cause? Did they suddenly become unavailable or overwhelmed with other obligations? Did they go still and distant in a way that felt like watching someone leave without moving? Or did they seem too perfect, too agreeable, too attuned to your every wish? You do not need to diagnose anything. You just need to start matching what you see to the framework you now have.

The Window Keeps Shifting

Psychiatrist Daniel Siegel introduced the concept of the **window of tolerance** to describe the zone of emotional and physiological arousal in which a person can function effectively (Siegel, 2012). Inside the window, a person can think clearly, respond proportionately, and engage with other people in a grounded way. Above the window, the sympathetic system takes over: agitation, reactivity, panic. Below the window, the dorsal vagal system takes over: numbness, disconnection, collapse.

For most people, the window of tolerance is wide enough to absorb the normal stresses of daily life. A frustrating email does not send them into a rage. A sad movie does not shut them down for the rest of the evening. They may feel their mood shift, but they stay within a range where they can recover quickly.

For a person with Complex PTSD, the window of tolerance is narrower. Sometimes much narrower. And it shifts. A good night's sleep, a calm morning, and a sense of safety can widen it considerably. A poor night's sleep, a stressful workday, or an approaching anniversary of something painful can shrink it to almost nothing. This is why your partner can seem perfectly fine on Tuesday and completely overwhelmed on Wednesday by the exact same type of conversation. Their capacity to stay regulated is not fixed. It moves with conditions that may be invisible to you and, sometimes, to them.

This is not an excuse for harmful behavior. It is an explanation for inconsistency. And understanding it will save you from the trap of thinking that because your partner handled something well last week, their inability to handle it this week means they are being difficult on purpose.

Romance Itself Sounds the Alarm

Here is the paradox that sits at the center of every new relationship with a Complex PTSD survivor. The thing you are offering, love, closeness, attention, care, is precisely the thing that activates their alarm system.

This makes no logical sense until you remember where Complex PTSD comes from. The original harm happened inside a relationship, usually with a caregiver. The child needed love from that person. The child also experienced pain from that person. The brain filed both experiences together: love and danger in the same folder. Decades later, when a new partner offers genuine warmth, the nervous system opens that folder and finds the old warning right next to the new feeling. The body cannot tell the difference between then and now. It only knows that this sensation, being close to someone, being needed by someone, has been dangerous before (Herman, 1992).

This is why your partner may pull away after a wonderful evening. This is why they may shut down after telling you something personal. This is why the relationship can feel like it takes two steps forward and one step back on a good week, and two steps back on a hard one. The closeness is not failing. The closeness is working. And working means activating everything the nervous system has stored about what closeness has cost in the past.

Their Body Decides Before Their Mind Does

Stephen Porges coined the term **neuroception** to describe the process by which the nervous system evaluates safety and danger below the level of conscious awareness (Porges, 2011). You do not decide to feel safe. Your body decides for you, based on cues so subtle that your conscious mind may never register them: a tone of voice, a facial micro-expression, the speed at which someone moves toward you, the feeling of a room.

For a person with Complex PTSD, neuroception is tuned to a setting that detects threat in places where none may be present. A raised eyebrow reads as disapproval. A pause before answering reads as withdrawal. A hand reaching toward them reads, for one fraction of a second, as something it is not. The conscious mind may know, a moment later, that you were reaching for the salt. But the body already responded. The heart rate jumped. The muscles tensed. The internal alarm sounded. And by the time your partner's thinking brain catches up with their survival brain, the damage to the moment has already been done.

This is not something your partner can simply decide to stop doing. Neuroception operates beneath choice. It can be recalibrated over time through consistent safe experiences, through therapy, and through the kind of patient, steady relational environment that we will discuss in Chapter 10. But in the early months of dating, you are working with a nervous system that has years of practice reading danger into safety. Your job is not to override that system. Your job is to understand it well enough that you stop taking its outputs personally.

The next time your partner's mood shifts suddenly, before you ask what went wrong, ask yourself a different question: What is their body responding to right now? You may not know the answer. But asking the question, instead of assuming the answer is about you, is the single most useful shift you can make.

Key Takeaways

Your partner's confusing behaviors in early dating are, in most cases, not choices. They are nervous system responses, produced by a body that learned to detect danger in closeness long before you arrived.

Four survival responses show up in dating: fight (sudden sharpness or defensiveness), flight (canceling, avoiding, disappearing), freeze (going blank, dissociating, shutting down), and fawn (over-accommodating, mirroring, performing the perfect partner). Your partner may move between several of these in a single evening.

The window of tolerance, the zone in which your partner can stay regulated and present, is narrower and less stable than most people's. It shifts with sleep, stress, and invisible factors you may never see.

Romance itself activates the alarm system, because Complex PTSD was caused by harm inside relationships, and your partner's nervous system has filed love and danger in the same place.

Their body decides before their mind does. A process called neuroception evaluates safety and threat below conscious awareness, and in Complex PTSD, that process is tuned to detect danger that may not be there. Understanding this will not fix the pattern, but it will change how you respond to it.

Chapter 3 The Push-Pull Is Not a Game

Mateo had never experienced anything like the first two months with Ines. She was magnetic, warm, and disarmingly open. On their second date, she told him she felt safer with him than she had felt with anyone in years. On their third, she reached for his hand across the table and said, "I want you to know I'm serious about this." Mateo, who had spent the previous two years in a series of flat, going-nowhere relationships, felt like he had finally found someone who matched his intensity.

Then Ines disappeared.

Not literally. She did not change her number or move cities. But over the course of a single week, she went from texting him throughout the day to responding with one-word messages twelve hours apart. She canceled their Friday plans, saying she needed a night to herself. When Mateo suggested rescheduling for Saturday, she said maybe. The maybe turned into silence. By Sunday night, Mateo was sitting on his kitchen floor scrolling through their earlier messages, trying to find the moment where everything shifted.

He could not find it, because there was no single moment. The shift was not about anything Mateo had said or done. It was about a nervous system doing exactly what it was designed to do: pulling away from closeness once closeness began to feel like a threat.

When Ines resurfaced four days later, she was warm again. Affectionate. She acted as though nothing had happened, and when Mateo asked, cautiously, if everything was okay, she said she had just been stressed with work. They went out that weekend and it was wonderful. The following Tuesday, she told him she was falling in love with him. By Thursday, she had gone quiet again.

Mateo did not know the word for what he was experiencing, but if you are reading this chapter, you probably do. The push-pull cycle is the single most reported source of distress for partners of people with Complex PTSD, and it is the pattern most likely to make a reasonable person feel like they are losing their mind. It is not a game. It is not a test. And understanding its mechanics is the difference between feeding the cycle and finding your way through it.

Two Needs That Cannot Share a Room

At the heart of the push-pull pattern is a specific type of attachment researchers call **disorganized attachment** (Main & Hesse, 1990). In secure attachment, a person has learned that closeness is safe and that the people they depend on will be reliably available. In anxious attachment, a person craves closeness but worries constantly about losing it. In avoidant attachment, a person values independence and pulls back from too much intimacy. Each of these styles has a consistent internal logic.

Disorganized attachment has no consistent logic, and that is precisely the problem. A person with disorganized attachment carries two opposing needs with equal force: the need for closeness and the terror of it. These two needs do not take turns. They operate simultaneously. The person reaches for connection because they are human and connection is a fundamental requirement, and then their nervous system floods with alarm because their earliest experiences taught them that the people they reach for are the people who cause the most pain.

This is the engine behind every push-pull cycle you have experienced with your partner. They are not alternating between wanting you and not wanting you. They want you all the time. And they are afraid of you all the time. Both things are true at once, and neither one is about you personally. It is about what closeness has cost them before.

As we discussed in Chapter 2, your partner's nervous system was calibrated by years of relational harm. Disorganized attachment is what happens when the calibration affects the attachment system specifically, leaving your partner in a constant state of approach and retreat that they may not even be able to explain to themselves.

The Cycle Has a Map

The push-pull pattern feels chaotic, but it follows a sequence that you can learn to recognize. Understanding the sequence will not eliminate it, but it will help you stop reacting from confusion and start responding from awareness.

The first phase is approach. During this phase, your partner moves toward you. They are open, warm, present, and available. The connection feels real because it is real. They are not performing. They are genuinely experiencing safety with you, and their nervous system is allowing closeness.

The second phase is activation. Something shifts. It may be a specific moment, a compliment that felt too intimate, a plan that implied a future together, a physical touch that crossed from comfortable to vulnerable. Or it may be nothing visible at all. The nervous system, which was tolerating closeness, reaches its limit. As we covered in Chapter 2, the window of tolerance has an upper edge, and your partner just hit it. The alarm sounds internally. Closeness, which felt good a moment ago, now registers as dangerous.

The third phase is withdrawal. Your partner pulls away. This may look like silence, emotional flatness, cancellation of plans, a sudden need to be alone, irritability, or a vague excuse that does not quite make sense. Oscar experienced this repeatedly with Eloise. After every particularly close weekend together, she would become unreachable by Monday evening. His texts would go unanswered. His calls would go to voicemail. When he asked mutual friends if she was okay, they said she seemed fine. She was fine, in the sense that nothing external had changed. What had changed was her internal state. Her body had decided that the level of closeness they had reached was not safe, and withdrawal was the only available relief.

The fourth phase is guilt and shame. After the withdrawal, your partner becomes aware, sometimes slowly, sometimes all at once, that they have pulled away from someone who was being kind to them. This awareness does not produce a clean correction. It produces shame. They feel defective for being unable to handle something that seems so simple. They may feel angry at themselves, or angry at you for wanting something they cannot consistently provide. This phase is usually invisible to the partner, because it happens inside your partner's head, but it is the fuel for the fifth phase.

The fifth phase is re-approach. Your partner comes back. They may be warmer than before, more attentive, more affectionate, as if compensating for the absence. The relief you feel during this phase is enormous, and it is also the most dangerous moment in the cycle, because the intensity of the reunion can create a false sense of resolution. Nothing has been resolved. The cycle has simply returned to its starting position.

Marcel learned to map this cycle with his partner by keeping a simple log. For three weeks, he tracked the moments when his partner moved toward him and the moments when she pulled away. The pattern was remarkably consistent: three to four days of closeness, followed by one to three days of distance, followed by a warm return. Once Marcel could see the pattern, he stopped interpreting each withdrawal as a crisis and started seeing it as a predictable phase with a beginning and an end. This did not make the withdrawals pleasant. But it made them survivable.

Try this yourself. Over the next two weeks, notice the rhythm of closeness and distance in your relationship. Do not try to change it. Do not confront your partner about it. Just observe and record. You are building a map of something that has felt unmappable, and the map itself is a form of power.

Know the Difference Between Pain and Manipulation

This section requires honesty, because the question deserves a direct answer. How do you tell the difference between a push-pull pattern driven by trauma and a push-pull pattern driven by manipulation?

The distinction matters. Trauma-driven push-pull is involuntary, distressing to the person doing it, and not designed to produce a specific outcome. Your partner is not withdrawing to punish you, test your loyalty, or increase your desire. They are withdrawing because their nervous system demanded it. They are usually confused and ashamed about their own behavior, and they would stop if they could.

Manipulation-driven push-pull is strategic, even if not fully conscious. The person withdraws to create anxiety, to see if you will chase, to maintain a power imbalance, or to condition you to accept less. There is no shame afterward, or the shame is performed rather than felt. The cycle is calibrated to produce a specific effect: keeping you off-balance and emotionally dependent.

Here are the signals that point toward trauma rather than manipulation. Your partner is distressed by their own pattern. They acknowledge, even if they cannot explain, that their behavior does not match their feelings. They do not enjoy the pursuit. They are not energized by your anxiety. And when they return, they are genuinely relieved, not triumphant.

Here are the signals that point in the other direction. Your partner seems comfortable with your distress. They respond to your confusion with dismissiveness rather than remorse. The cycle consistently results in you doing more emotional work while they do less. They resist any conversation about the pattern itself. And you feel worse about yourself over time, not just confused.

Most readers of this book will recognize the first set of signals. If you recognize the second set, the issue may not be Complex PTSD, or it may be Complex PTSD combined with patterns that are genuinely harmful to you. Chapter 9 will address this distinction in full, because the question of when to stay and when to go requires more than a single section to answer well.

Your Attachment Style Is Part of the Equation

The push-pull cycle does not operate in a vacuum. Your nervous system is responding to theirs, and theirs is responding to yours, and the interaction between your two attachment styles can either dampen the cycle or amplify it.

If you lean toward anxious attachment, the withdrawal phase of the cycle will activate your deepest fears. You will want to pursue: send more texts, ask more questions, show up unannounced, demand reassurance. Every instinct will tell you to close the gap. But pursuing a partner whose nervous system just declared closeness dangerous will push them further away. Your pursuit confirms their alarm. The harder you chase, the faster they run, and the faster they run, the harder you chase. This is the anxious-disorganized spiral, and it can escalate a manageable pattern into a destructive one within weeks.

If you lean toward avoidant attachment, the withdrawal phase may activate your own impulse to pull back. When your partner retreats, you may match their distance and add to it, rationalizing that you are giving them space when you are actually protecting yourself. When they return during the re-approach phase, you may be slower to engage, guarded by the memory of the last withdrawal. This creates a different kind of spiral, one in which both partners orbit at increasing distance until the relationship quietly dies of starvation.

The most helpful position during the push-pull cycle is neither pursuit nor retreat. It is steady presence. You remain reachable without chasing. You give space without disappearing. You communicate warmth without demanding a response. This is simple to describe and extraordinarily difficult to practice, which is why the script bank below may be the most useful tool in this chapter.

When your partner pulls away, instead of texting four times in increasing urgency, try something like this: "I'm here when you're ready. No rush." When they return, instead of pretending nothing happened or launching into a discussion about what went wrong, try: "I'm glad you're back. I missed you." These responses accomplish something crucial. They tell your partner's nervous system that closeness does not come with a penalty for leaving, and that returning is safe.

Stay Without Chasing, Leave Without Abandoning

The phrase "not chasing and not abandoning" is easy to say and profoundly hard to live. In practical terms, it means holding a position that neither feeds the cycle nor cuts it off. It means tolerating your own discomfort during the withdrawal phase without making it your partner's problem. It means staying present without being invasive, and giving space without being punitive.

Clara, whom we first met in Chapter 1, found her way to this position after the third cycle of closeness and distance with her partner. She wrote herself a set of rules on an index card and kept it on her nightstand. The rules were simple: During withdrawal, she would send one warm text per day, no more. She would not ask for explanations. She would not stalk social media. She would do one thing each day that was entirely about her own life, a meal with a friend, an hour of reading, a long walk. During the return, she would be warm but honest. She would say, "I'm glad to hear from you. It was hard not hearing from you." And she would not pretend the distance had not happened.

These rules did not fix the cycle. They gave Clara a way to live inside it without losing herself. And over time, as her partner experienced Clara's consistency, the withdrawal phases became shorter and the re-approach phases became calmer. The cycle did not disappear, but it became less extreme, because Clara's steady presence offered her partner's nervous system something it desperately needed: evidence that pulling away did not destroy the connection.

Key Takeaways

The push-pull cycle is the most distressing pattern for partners of Complex PTSD survivors, and it is not a game, a test, or a strategy. It is driven by disorganized attachment, in which the need for closeness and the fear of closeness operate simultaneously.

The cycle follows a predictable sequence: approach, activation, withdrawal, guilt and shame, and re-approach. Mapping this sequence in your own relationship will help you stop interpreting each phase as a crisis and start seeing it as a pattern with a rhythm you can learn.

The distinction between trauma-driven and manipulative push-pull is critical. Trauma-driven withdrawal is involuntary, distressing to your partner, and not designed to produce a specific outcome. Manipulative push-pull is strategic and benefits from your confusion.

Your own attachment style interacts with the cycle. Anxious partners tend to pursue, which accelerates the withdrawal. Avoidant partners tend to match the distance, which starves the connection. The most useful position is steady presence: reachable without chasing, giving space without vanishing.

Hold your ground. Stay warm. Let the cycle run without feeding it, and over time, your consistency can become the evidence your partner's nervous system needs to begin trusting that closeness is survivable.

Chapter 4 Landmines You Cannot See

Sebastian and Margot had been dating for two months, and the evening was going well. They were at her kitchen table, eating pasta he had made, talking about a trip they might take in the spring. He was mid-sentence, describing a hotel he had stayed at years ago, when he leaned across the table to refill her wine glass. He reached past her, his arm crossing her line of vision, and Margot stopped breathing.

Her hand closed around her fork so tightly her knuckles went white. Her eyes dropped to the table. Sebastian, noticing the silence, pulled his arm back and asked if she was okay. She nodded, but her voice had changed. For the rest of the evening, she spoke in short, flat sentences, like someone reading a script for a role she no longer wanted to play.

Sebastian left that night certain he had done something wrong, but unable to identify what. He replayed the evening in his mind. The food had been good. The conversation had been easy. He had not said anything unkind or controversial. The only thing that had changed was the moment he reached for the wine bottle, and he could not understand how a gesture that simple could have ended the evening.

What Sebastian did not know was that Margot's father had been a large man who used his physical presence to intimidate. An arm crossing her line of sight, a body leaning into her space with sudden movement, could activate a response so deep and so fast that Margot's conscious mind could not catch up to it. She did not think about her father at that table. She did not see a memory. She felt a sensation, a full-body contraction of alarm and helplessness, that arrived without warning and left her stranded inside her own skin for the rest of the night.

This chapter is about the invisible activations that can turn a perfectly ordinary moment into something your partner's body reads as a crisis. Understanding what these activations are, how they differ from ordinary emotional reactions, and what you can do when they happen will change the way you move through every shared evening, every conversation, and every moment of silence that follows.

What a Nervous System Activation Actually Is

The word most people use for what Margot experienced has been stretched so far in popular conversation that it has lost much of its clinical meaning. In clinical terms, a nervous system activation occurs when a sensory, emotional, or situational cue connects to a stored traumatic memory and produces an involuntary physiological response (Van der Kolk, 2014). The cue does not need to resemble the original harm in any obvious way. It only needs to share one element, a sound, a smell, a body position, a tone of voice, a specific word, with something the nervous system filed as dangerous.

This is why the activations in your relationship will often seem to come from nowhere. You are not doing anything wrong. You are doing something that shares one invisible thread with a past experience your partner may not even consciously remember. Their body remembers, and their body responds before any thought can intervene.

As we explored in Chapter 2, the process called neuroception operates below conscious awareness. Your partner's body evaluates cues for safety and danger at a speed that bypasses rational thought (Porges, 2011). By the time your partner can think about what is happening, the physiological response has already begun. Their heart rate has changed. Their muscles have tensed or gone slack. Their breathing has shifted. And the emotional state that follows, fear, shame, rage, or a hollow numbness, feels absolutely real and absolutely present, even though it was generated by something that is not present at all.

Emotional Flashbacks Have No Picture

One of the most important concepts in Complex PTSD, and one of the least understood outside clinical circles, is the **emotional flashback**. Pete Walker distinguished emotional flashbacks from the visual flashbacks most people associate with PTSD (Walker, 2013). In a visual flashback, a person sees images or scenes from a traumatic event. In an emotional flashback, a person is suddenly overwhelmed by the emotions of a past traumatic experience, with no visual memory attached.

This distinction matters enormously for dating, because emotional flashbacks are invisible to the person experiencing them and to everyone around them. There is no moment where your partner says, "I am remembering something." There is no sudden gasp or glazed stare at a memory. There is only a shift: a wave of shame, fear, rage, helplessness, or abandonment terror that crashes through their body without a label or an explanation.

Hugo saw this clearly one evening when he and Lucia were discussing where to spend Christmas. The conversation was calm. They were looking at calendars, talking about logistics. Then Hugo said, casually, "I just think it would be nice to spend it together this year." Lucia's face crumpled. Her eyes filled with tears. She left the room without a word and sat in the bathroom for twenty minutes. When she came out, she said she did not know why she was crying. She was not sad. She was not angry. She genuinely did not know what had happened.

What had happened was that the phrase "spend it together" activated a cascade of emotions from holidays in Lucia's childhood, holidays that had been marked by her mother's unpredictable rage and the loneliness of trying to celebrate in a house that felt more like a prison than a home. Lucia did not see those holidays. She did not think about her mother. She felt the feelings of a child who had learned that together meant trapped, and the feelings arrived with such force that they swallowed whatever she was actually feeling about Hugo and his perfectly reasonable Christmas suggestion.

If your partner experiences something like this, and if you are in the early months of dating someone with Complex PTSD, they almost certainly will, the most important thing you can know is this: they are not reacting to you. They are reacting to a recording that your present-moment cue pressed play on. And the recording is playing at full volume inside a body that cannot find the pause button.

The Ordinary Things That Sound the Alarm

In early dating, certain types of moments are more likely to produce nervous system activations than others. Knowing what they are will not prevent them, but it will help you stop blaming yourself when they occur.

Certain tones of voice, particularly tones that carry authority, impatience, or disappointment, can produce immediate responses. Your partner's body may be calibrated to detect parental disapproval in vocal frequencies you do not even notice. Coralie told her therapist that her partner's voice, when he was tired, dropped into a register that sounded exactly like her stepfather's voice before he became angry. Her partner was not angry. He was exhausted. But her body could not tell the difference.

The transition from public space to private space is another common activation point. A restaurant, a park, a movie theater: these are environments with witnesses, implicit safety, and easy exits. A car, an apartment, a bedroom: these are enclosed, private, and associated with the places where childhood harm most often occurred. Your partner may be relaxed and present during dinner and become tense and distant the moment you walk through the front door together. This is not about your home. It is about what private space has meant before.

Relationship milestones carry activation potential because they represent increased commitment and decreased escape routes. Meeting your friends. Meeting your family. Exchanging keys. Discussing exclusivity. Using the word love. Each of these is a door that, once opened, is harder to close, and for a person whose survival has depended on keeping exit routes available, each one can produce a disproportionate stress response.

Physical touch that is unexpected, that crosses from one body zone to another (from arm to face, from hand to waist), or that occurs from behind can activate responses tied to physical harm or sexual abuse. Your partner may be perfectly comfortable holding your hand and become rigid the moment your hand moves to the small of their back. The difference between the two touches may seem negligible to you. To their nervous system, it is the difference between a known quantity and an unknown one, and the unknown has been dangerous before.

The Right Question Is Not "What's Wrong?"

When your partner's mood shifts suddenly and you can see that something has changed, the instinct to ask "What's wrong?" is natural and nearly universal. It is also, in most activation situations, the least helpful thing you can say.

"What's wrong?" asks your partner to identify and articulate the source of their distress in real time. But during an emotional flashback or a nervous system activation, the thinking parts of the brain are partially offline. Your partner may genuinely not know what is wrong. Asking them to explain puts them in a position of having to produce an answer their neurology cannot currently generate, which adds shame and frustration on top of the activation itself.

Better alternatives share a common quality: they offer presence without demanding performance.

"I'm here" communicates availability without requiring a response. "Take whatever time you need" communicates patience without creating pressure to recover on a schedule. "You seem like you're having a hard moment. I'm not going anywhere" communicates steadiness and removes the threat of abandonment. "We do not need to talk about it right now" removes the expectation of immediate processing.

Felix learned this after a difficult evening with his partner. He had asked "What's wrong?" three times in five minutes, and each time his partner became more withdrawn. When he finally stopped asking and simply sat quietly next to her without speaking, she reached for his hand twenty minutes later. The silence had been almost unbearable for Felix. It had been exactly what her nervous system needed.

Co-Regulation for Beginners

When your partner is activated, their nervous system is looking for signals of safety. This is where a concept called **co-regulation** becomes relevant. Co-regulation is the process by which one person's calm nervous system helps another person's activated nervous system return to baseline (Porges, 2011). It is not a technique you perform. It is a state you maintain.

The fundamentals are simpler than you might expect. First, regulate your own body. If you are anxious, frustrated, or frightened by what you are seeing, your body will broadcast those signals and your partner's nervous system will pick them up. Slow your breathing. Drop your shoulders. Soften your face. You are not pretending to be calm. You are deliberately calming your own system so that yours can communicate safety to theirs.

Second, reduce sensory input. If the room is loud, lower the volume or move to a quieter space. If the lights are bright, dim them. If there are other people around, offer to step away together or give your partner the option to step away alone. An activated nervous system is already processing too much information. Reducing the load helps.

Third, match their energy without matching their distress. If your partner has gone quiet, be quiet with them. If they need to move, walk with them. Do not try to shift their energy by being cheerful, making jokes, or changing the subject to something lighter. These strategies, while well-intentioned, send the message that their current state is unacceptable and needs to be fixed immediately.

Fourth, wait. Co-regulation is not a thirty-second process. It can take minutes or, in some cases, much longer for an activated nervous system to return to a state where conversation and connection are possible again. Your willingness to wait, without commentary, without visible impatience, is itself a signal of safety.

Practice this once before you need it. Sit quietly, slow your breathing, and notice what it feels like to bring your own body into a calm state deliberately. The more familiar you are with your own regulation process, the more reliably you will be able to access it when your partner's nervous system is asking for help.

Key Takeaways

A nervous system activation occurs when a present-moment cue connects to stored traumatic material and produces an involuntary physiological response. The cue often shares only one element with the original harm, which is why activations can seem to come from nowhere.

Emotional flashbacks, a concept from Pete Walker's work, involve being flooded by the emotions of past trauma without any visual memory. Your partner may not know what they are feeling or why, and asking them to explain in the moment usually makes it worse.

Common early-dating activations include certain tones of voice, the transition from public to private space, relationship milestones, and unexpected physical touch. Knowing these patterns will help you stop blaming yourself for responses that are not about you.

Replace "What's wrong?" with statements that offer presence without demanding performance: "I'm here," "Take your time," "We do not need to talk about it right now."

Co-regulation, the process by which your calm nervous system helps your partner's activated nervous system return to baseline, is the most practical skill you can develop for these moments. It begins with regulating yourself, reducing sensory input, matching your partner's energy without matching their distress, and waiting with patience you may not feel but can learn to practice.

Chapter 5 The Disclosure Conversation

Valeria told Gabriel on a park bench on a Sunday afternoon in March. They had been dating for three months. She had planned the conversation in her head for weeks, rehearsed the wording in the shower, and chosen the park because it was public, which felt safer than his apartment, and because she could leave easily if she needed to.

She started by saying, "I need to tell you something about my past." Gabriel put down his coffee and turned to face her. She told him, in careful, measured sentences, that she had been abused by a family member for several years as a child. She did not give details. She did not name the person. She said the words as though she were reading them from a card she had memorized, and her hands shook the entire time.

Gabriel did not speak for about ten seconds after she finished. Then he said, "I'm so sorry that happened to you." Then he said, "Thank you for telling me." Then he asked if she wanted to talk about it more or if she wanted to change the subject. Valeria said she wanted to change the subject. They talked about the ducks on the pond for a while, and then they walked to a bakery and shared a pastry, and the rest of the afternoon was quiet and warm.

That evening, Valeria texted him: "I was terrified to tell you. You made it okay. I just wanted you to know that."

Gabriel did not realize it at the time, but his response on that bench had been nearly perfect. Not because he had said anything brilliant, but because he had done three things right: he had listened without reacting dramatically, he had followed her lead on how far to go, and he had made the rest of the afternoon feel normal. In a moment that could have reshaped their relationship for the worse, his steadiness allowed it to reshape for the better.

This chapter is about the moment when your partner's past enters your present. It may happen the way it happened for Gabriel, in a planned conversation with careful words. It may happen entirely differently. What matters is that you understand the forms disclosure can take, what your partner is risking when they share, and how your response in that moment will echo through every month that follows.

Three Ways the Past Enters the Room

Disclosure in early dating almost never looks like a single, complete conversation. It tends to arrive in one of three forms, and knowing which one you are in will help you respond well.

The first is the planned disclosure, the one Valeria gave Gabriel. Your partner has decided, after considerable internal debate, to tell you something specific about their history. They have chosen the moment, rehearsed the words, and braced themselves for your reaction. Planned disclosures tend to be brief, carefully worded, and emotionally controlled on the surface. Underneath, your partner is terrified. They are watching your face for micro-expressions of disgust, pity, or the kind of shock that signals this is too much for you to handle.

The second is the accidental reveal. This is the disclosure that happens without planning, often through a nervous system activation like the ones we discussed in Chapter 4. Noemi experienced this when Julian woke up from a nightmare beside her at four in the morning, gasping and disoriented, and could not stop talking for twenty minutes about things she had never heard before. He was not choosing to disclose. His body had broken through a wall that his conscious mind had been maintaining, and the information came out raw, unfiltered, and overwhelming for both of them. Accidental reveals are harder to manage because neither partner is prepared, and the emotional intensity is uncontrolled.

The third is the slow leak. This is the most common form in early dating, and it is the easiest to miss if you are not paying attention. Your partner does not sit you down and tell you a story. Instead, fragments surface over weeks or months. An offhand comment about not liking a certain neighborhood because "something happened there once." A passing mention of an uncle they do not speak to. A joke about their childhood that is too dark to be funny. A flinch when you reach for them a certain way. Each piece is small enough to dismiss, but together they form a picture that your partner may or may not intend for you to see.

Ines used the slow-leak method with Mateo for nearly four months before either of them acknowledged what was being communicated. One evening, after she made a comment about hating the smell of whiskey because "it reminds me of someone I'd rather forget," Mateo said, gently, "You've mentioned things like this a few times. I don't need to know more than you want to tell me, but I want you to know that I'm listening, and none of it changes how I feel about you." Ines cried. She later told him that his words had made her feel seen in a way she had been afraid to ask for.

What They Are Risking When They Tell You

Understanding what disclosure costs your partner will help you receive it with the weight it deserves. When a person with Complex PTSD shares any piece of their trauma history, they are putting several things on the table at once.

They are risking rejection. The belief that they are damaged goods, too broken for a real relationship, is a core feature of Complex PTSD, as we discussed in Chapter 1. Disclosure is, at its deepest level, a test of that belief. They are showing you the part of themselves they are most convinced will drive you away, and they are waiting to see if it does.

They are risking being redefined. Before disclosure, your partner was a person you were getting to know, with all the complexity and possibility that implies. After disclosure, they fear becoming a label in your mind: a victim, a survivor, someone to be handled with kid gloves. They do not want your pity. Many do not even want your sympathy. They want what they wanted before they told you: to be seen as a whole person, not a diagnosis.

They are risking loss of control. Trauma removes control. Disclosure, even when planned, recreates a version of that vulnerability. By telling you, they are giving you information they cannot take back, and they are trusting you not to use it against them, share it without permission, or bring it up at the wrong moment. For someone whose core wound is about betrayal by trusted people, this is an act of enormous courage.

They are risking the relationship itself. Paloma told Gabriel (before Valeria was in the picture) about a difficult period in her life, and the man she had been dating at the time responded by saying, "That explains a lot about you." He meant it kindly. She heard it as confirmation that she was a case study, not a partner. The relationship ended within two weeks. One sentence, delivered without care, had turned disclosure into a wound.

How to Receive What You Are Given

There is no perfect script for receiving your partner's disclosure. There is, however, a set of principles that will serve you well regardless of the form the disclosure takes.

First, do not perform. Do not gasp. Do not cry on their behalf. Do not put your hand over your mouth. Do not say, "Oh my God." Your partner has rehearsed this moment in their mind dozens of times, and in many of those rehearsals, your dramatic reaction is exactly what made them decide not to tell you. Dramatic responses center your feelings in a moment that belongs to them.

Second, do not minimize. "It could have been worse" is never helpful. "At least you're okay now" dismisses the ongoing effects of something that is, by definition, not over. "Everyone has a tough childhood" erases the specificity of their experience. Minimizing is often an attempt to reduce your own discomfort. Resist it.

Third, do not investigate. Your curiosity is natural, but this is not the moment to satisfy it. Do not ask for details about what happened, who did it, how long it lasted, or how they feel about the person who harmed them. If they wanted to tell you those things, they would. Your restraint communicates something powerful: that you can be trusted with partial information without demanding more.

Fourth, follow their lead. If they want to keep talking, listen. If they want to stop, stop. If they want to act as though nothing happened and go back to discussing dinner plans, go back to discussing dinner plans. The pace of this conversation belongs to them, and your willingness to match it is one of the most respectful things you can offer.

Fifth, say something simple and true. The most effective responses to disclosure are short. "Thank you for telling me." "I'm glad you trust me with this." "This does not change how I feel about you." "I'm here." These sentences work because they affirm without interpreting, and they close the vulnerability loop without demanding that it stay open.

Hugo, who by this point had been dating Lucia for several months, received an accidental disclosure during a difficult evening. Lucia, in the grip of an emotional flashback, said things about her childhood that she had never said aloud before. When it was over, Hugo said, "I heard everything you said. I am not going anywhere. You can tell me more whenever you want, or never. Both are fine." He later told a friend that he had felt completely out of his depth in that moment, that he had no idea if he was saying the right things, and that his hands were shaking. Lucia never knew his hands were shaking. She only knew that he stayed.

After your partner has disclosed, take some time to check in with yourself. Notice what you felt in your body while they were speaking. Notice what thoughts arose. Notice what impulses you had, to fix, to comfort, to flee, to research, to call someone and tell them what you just heard. All of these impulses are information about your own nervous system and your own relational patterns. You do not need to act on any of them immediately. But noticing them is the beginning of understanding how disclosure affects you, not just your partner. You will carry this information too, and how you carry it matters. We will return to this in Chapter 8, when we turn the mirror on your own history and your own responses.

The Conversation That Happens in Pieces

Healthy disclosure is not a single event. It is an ongoing process that unfolds in layers over weeks, months, and sometimes years. Therapist Lindsay Braman uses the term **tiered disclosure** to describe this process, in which a person shares progressively deeper information as trust builds (Braman, 2021).

The first tier is general. "I had a difficult childhood." "My family situation was complicated." "There are some things from my past that still affect me." These statements signal the presence of a story without revealing its contents. They are an invitation for you to demonstrate that you can hold space for complexity.

The second tier adds shape. "I grew up with a parent who was unpredictable." "I was in a relationship that was harmful." "Something happened to me that I've been working through in therapy." These statements give you enough information to understand the general territory without mapping the specific terrain.

The third tier includes specific events, people, and impacts. This level of disclosure usually appears only after significant trust has been established, and it may not appear for months or longer. Some partners never reach the third tier verbally, and that is entirely within their right.

Your role across all tiers is the same: receive what is given, do not press for what is not, and let your partner set the pace. Each time they share a piece and find that you handle it with care, they build a data point for safety. Over time, those data points accumulate into something their nervous system can begin to trust.

When No One Says Anything at All

There is a fourth scenario that the three-part framework above does not cover, and it is one of the most common in early dating: your partner has not disclosed anything, but the behavioral evidence is clear. The emotional flashbacks, the push-pull pattern, the nervous system activations, the flinch when you move too quickly, all of these have been present, and neither of you has named what they point to.

This situation is delicate. You may be fairly certain that your partner has a trauma history. You may have done enough reading (including the previous chapters of this book) to recognize the patterns. But naming someone else's experience for them, particularly when it involves trauma, is territory that requires extreme care.

You cannot diagnose your partner. You should not tell them you think they have Complex PTSD. You should not present your observations as conclusions about their psychology. What you can do is describe what you see, without interpreting it, and open a door they can walk through if they choose to.

A sentence like this can work: "I've noticed that sometimes after we're really close, you seem to need a lot of space. I want you to know that I'm not going anywhere, and if there's anything you'd like me to understand about what that's about, I'm ready to listen." This sentence does three things: it names an observable pattern, it removes the threat of abandonment, and it offers an invitation without a demand. Your partner may not respond to it right away. They may not respond to it at all. But the door is open, and knowing the door is there, knowing that you see them and are not running, may be enough to let them begin.

Key Takeaways

Disclosure in early dating takes three primary forms: the planned conversation, the accidental reveal during a moment of activation, and the slow leak of fragments over time. Each form requires a different kind of attention, but the core principles are the same.

Your partner is risking rejection, redefinition, loss of control, and the relationship itself when they share any part of their history. Understanding the weight of what they are offering will help you receive it well.

The best responses to disclosure are simple, short, and true. Do not perform shock. Do not minimize. Do not press for details. Follow their lead, and say something that affirms without interpreting.

Healthy disclosure happens in tiers, not all at once. Each layer builds trust, and trust is what allows the next layer to emerge. Your patience with this process is not passive. It is an active contribution to your partner's sense of safety.

When no disclosure has been given but the patterns are visible, you can name what you observe and open a door. You cannot push your partner through it. But knowing the door is there may be the thing that makes it possible for them to walk through on their own time.

Chapter 6 Touch, Intimacy, and the Body That Remembers

The first time Mateo stayed overnight at Ines's apartment, everything was going well until it was not. They had been dating for nearly three months. The evening had been relaxed. Dinner, a film, a slow shift from the couch to the bedroom that felt mutual and unforced. Ines was present and warm. She kissed him. She pulled him closer. There was no hesitation in her, and Mateo felt, for the first time, that they were moving past the careful, measured early weeks into something deeper.

Then, in the middle of a moment that should have been close and connected, Ines went still. Her body did not tense. It did the opposite. It went slack, as if someone had pulled a plug. Her eyes were open but unfocused. Her breathing became so shallow it was almost invisible. Mateo said her name. She did not respond. He said it again, louder, and touched her shoulder. She blinked, looked at him as though trying to place where she was, and said, "I think I need a minute."

She went to the bathroom and stayed there for twenty minutes. When she came back, she apologized four times, said she did not know what had happened, and asked if he wanted to leave. Mateo did not want to leave. He wanted to understand. But he also felt, in his own body, a disorienting mix of concern, confusion, and a guilt he could not name. Had he done something wrong? Had he missed a signal? Had he pushed past something she had not been ready for?

He had not. What Mateo witnessed was a freeze response during physical intimacy, the kind of shutdown described in Chapter 2, occurring in the specific context where trauma stored in the body is most likely to surface. Ines's conscious mind had wanted to be close to him. Her body had a different set of instructions, written years earlier, and in the moment when vulnerability was highest, those older instructions overrode everything else.

This chapter addresses the dimension of early dating that produces the most anxiety for both partners: the progression of physical closeness when one person carries a trauma history in their body. It is a chapter about consent, about patience, about the difference between desire and safety, and about the practical steps that can make physical intimacy possible without making it a minefield.

The Body Keeps Its Own Records

The clinical literature on trauma and the body has established, with considerable evidence, that traumatic experiences are stored not only as memories in the brain but as patterns in the body itself (Van der Kolk, 2014). Muscles remember. Skin remembers. The nervous system remembers. And these body-level memories can be activated by sensory cues that the conscious mind does not register: a particular pressure, a specific position, a temperature, the weight of another person's body.

This is why your partner may be fully consenting, fully willing, and fully present in their thinking mind, and still experience a physiological response that contradicts all of that. As we discussed in Chapter 4, neuroception operates below the level of conscious choice. During physical intimacy, when the body is at its most exposed and its most vulnerable, neuroception is running at its highest sensitivity. The body is scanning for danger in every touch, every shift of weight, every change in breathing rhythm. And if it finds something that matches a stored pattern, it responds.

The response may be a freeze, like what Mateo saw with Ines. It may be a fight response, a sudden irritability or physical rigidity that seems to come from nowhere. It may be a fawn response, in which your partner performs engagement and enthusiasm they do not feel because their nervous system has learned that compliance is safer than refusal. This last possibility is the one that deserves particular attention, because in the context of physical intimacy, fawning is the hardest pattern to detect and the most important to understand.

When Desire and Safety Are Not the Same Thing

Coralie recognized the pattern in herself six weeks into dating Oscar. She wanted to be physically close to him. She was attracted to him. And yet, every time they were together in that way, she noticed that she was performing. She was making sounds she thought he wanted to hear. She was positioning her body in ways she thought would please him. She was monitoring his responses more than she was experiencing her own. Afterward, she felt hollow, as though she had left the room during the act and was only now returning.

Coralie had spent years in a relationship where physical intimacy was not optional. She had learned that the safest way to manage it was to become whatever the other person wanted, to read their desires and reflect them back with precision, so that the experience would end more quickly and with less damage. That pattern did not disappear because Oscar was kind. It ran automatically, beneath conscious awareness, whenever her body registered the conditions associated with intimacy.

If your partner seems too eager, too accommodating, or too focused on your pleasure to the complete exclusion of their own, this may not be generosity. It may be the fawn response in its most intimate form. And the correction for it is not to confront your partner or to stop being physical entirely. The correction is to create an environment where not performing is safe, where a pause is welcomed rather than questioned, and where your partner's actual experience matters more than the appearance of a seamless encounter.

Consent as a Living Conversation

In most dating advice, consent is treated as a gate: you get permission, you pass through, you proceed. For early-stage relationships where one partner has Complex PTSD, consent needs to function differently. It is not a gate you pass through once. It is a conversation that stays open throughout the experience, because your partner's internal state can change rapidly and without warning.

This does not mean stopping every thirty seconds to ask clinical questions. It means building a shared language for checking in that feels natural rather than procedural.

Some couples use a traffic light system. Green means everything feels good, keep going. Yellow means something is shifting and a pause would help, not a stop, but a moment to recalibrate. Red means stop, no questions asked, no disappointment expressed, no negotiation. The simplicity of the system is its strength. Your partner does not need to explain what changed or why. They only need to say one word, and you respond accordingly.

Zoe and Elio developed their own version of this. Elio told Zoe early on that there might be moments where he needed to slow down, and he asked if they could agree on a way for him to signal that without it becoming a conversation in the moment. They settled on Elio placing his hand flat on Zoe's shoulder, a gentle, silent cue that meant "I need a minute." No drama. No explanation required. Zoe told him later that knowing the signal was in place made her feel safer too, because she was no longer afraid of accidentally causing harm without realizing it.

The action here is straightforward. Before physical intimacy progresses further in your relationship, have a calm conversation, fully clothed, at a table, with the lights on, about what each of you needs in order to feel safe. Ask your partner if there are types of touch, positions, or situations that are difficult for them. Ask if they have a way they prefer to signal that something needs to change. Offer your own signals as well. Making this conversation ordinary and collaborative, rather than clinical or heavy, removes the pressure and creates a framework you can both rely on when language is harder to access.

What Dissociation Looks Like Up Close

The freeze response during intimacy, the pattern Mateo saw with Ines, is one expression of dissociation, the process by which the mind disconnects from the present moment as a protective measure (Van der Kolk, 2014). Recognizing dissociation in your partner is important because it can be subtle, and because continuing physical contact with a person who has dissociated is harmful even when unintentional.

Signs of dissociation during physical closeness include a sudden stillness that feels different from relaxation, eyes that are open but unfocused or seem to be looking at something that is not in the room, a noticeable change in breathing (very shallow or very slow), a body that goes limp or rigid without explanation, responses that feel automatic rather than engaged, and a quality of absence, the sense that the person in front of you has gone somewhere else while their body remains.

If you notice any of these signs, stop. You do not need to make a dramatic gesture. Simply stop what you are doing, create a small amount of physical space (move your hands to a neutral position, shift your weight), and say something calm and grounding: "Hey, I'm right here. Take your time." Do not ask what happened. Do not express frustration or confusion. Do not touch them further until they re-engage on their own terms.

Mateo learned, over several more months with Ines, that the moments after dissociation were the most important ones. The first few times, he panicked. He asked too many questions. He tried to fix what he could not understand. Eventually, he learned that the most helpful thing he could do was lie beside her, not touching her, and wait. When she came back, she would reach for his hand. That small gesture, the reaching, told him everything he needed to know: she was present again, and she wanted him there.

Reconnection After a Difficult Moment

When a moment of physical intimacy goes sideways, the temptation is to avoid the subject entirely. This is understandable. Both partners feel raw. The person who experienced the activation may feel ashamed, broken, or afraid that they have ruined the relationship. The other partner may feel guilty, confused, or frightened by what they witnessed. Neither person wants to make things worse.

But silence after a rupture does not protect the relationship. It creates distance. And in early dating, where the foundation is still being built, distance after intimacy is especially corrosive.

The conversation does not need to happen in the moment. It should not happen in the moment. Give it a day. Then, in a calm setting, say something simple: "I wanted to check in about the other night. I care about you, and I want us to be able to talk about it when you're ready." Your partner may not be ready right away. That is their right. But the offer itself communicates something essential: that what happened did not scare you away, that you are not angry, and that the relationship can absorb difficult moments without collapsing.

Eloise told her therapist that the turning point in her relationship was not the night her partner handled a freeze response well. It was the morning after, when he made her coffee, sat down across from her, and said, "That was hard for both of us. I'm glad we're here this morning." No pressure. No processing. Just a statement that confirmed two things: it happened, and we survived it. That was enough to make the next time feel less terrifying.

In a Nutshell

Physical intimacy with a Complex PTSD survivor involves the body's stored trauma responses, which operate independently of conscious desire or consent. Your partner may want closeness and simultaneously experience a nervous system that reads closeness as danger.

The fawn response during intimacy, performing engagement that is not genuinely felt, is the hardest pattern to detect and the most important to watch for. An environment where pausing is welcomed and performance is unnecessary is the best protection against it.

Consent in this relationship is not a single gate you pass through. It is a conversation that stays open, supported by simple tools like the traffic light system or a nonverbal signal both partners agree on in advance.

Dissociation during intimacy is recognizable if you know what to look for: stillness, unfocused eyes, shallow breathing, a quality of absence. If you see it, stop, create space, and wait without commentary.

Reconnection after a difficult moment matters more than prevention. The conversation does not need to happen immediately, but it does need to happen. A simple check-in the next day, offered without pressure, tells your partner that the relationship can hold what happened without breaking.

Chapter 7 You Are Not Their Therapist

Clara did not notice it happening. It started small. Martin would have a hard evening, and Clara would stay up an extra hour talking him through it. He would cancel plans because he felt overwhelmed, and Clara would rearrange her schedule around his emotional state. He mentioned once that he found it hard to call therapists, so Clara researched five in their area, made a spreadsheet of their specialties and availability, and texted it to him with a heart emoji.

By the third month, Clara was reading two books on Complex PTSD, listening to a trauma-recovery podcast during her commute, and spending her lunch breaks in online forums for partners of trauma survivors. She knew more about the four survival responses than most graduate students. She could identify Martin's window of tolerance by the look on his face. She had developed a mental catalog of his activation points and could steer conversations away from them with a precision that impressed even her.

She was also exhausted. She had stopped going to her pottery class. She had not seen her closest friend in three weeks. She was sleeping poorly, checking her phone at two in the morning to see if Martin had texted about a nightmare. And when a colleague asked how her new relationship was going, Clara said, without irony, "It is a lot of work, but I feel like I am really helping him."

Clara was not in a relationship. She was running a one-woman treatment clinic, and she did not even know it.

The slide from partner to caretaker is the most common relational trap for people dating someone with Complex PTSD, and it begins with the best intentions. You see someone you care about struggling. You want to help. You have the capacity to help. And the help you provide feels meaningful, even necessary, which makes it almost impossible to see the moment when helping becomes the entire architecture of the relationship. This chapter is about recognizing that moment, understanding why it is harmful to both of you, and learning the difference between supporting someone's healing and becoming responsible for it.

The Caretaker Slide Starts with Empathy

The progression is predictable enough that it deserves a name. Call it the caretaker slide. It begins with empathy, a genuine emotional response to your partner's pain. Empathy leads to action: you research, you accommodate, you adjust. Action leads to routine: the researching and accommodating become regular parts of your week. Routine leads to identity: you begin to see yourself primarily through the lens of how well you are managing your partner's condition. And identity leads to depletion: you have given so much of yourself to the project of their healing that there is very little of you left over for anything else.

Margot recognized this pattern after Felix's fifth week of canceled plans. She had spent each of those weeks finding ways to make things easier for him: suggesting low-stimulation dates, texting him grounding reminders before social events, and pre-screening movies for content that might be difficult. When her sister asked her what she had done for fun that month, Margot could not answer. Everything she had done was in service of Felix's comfort. Her own comfort had become an afterthought.

The caretaker slide is seductive because it feels like love. In a culture that celebrates sacrifice and equates devotion with suffering, the partner who gives everything appears heroic. But the clinical reality is different. A relationship in which one partner absorbs the emotional labor of managing the other's mental health is not a partnership. It is a caregiving arrangement, and caregiving arrangements produce burnout, resentment, and a power imbalance that is harmful to both people involved.

Why the Dynamic Hurts Both of You

For you, the caretaker, the cost accumulates quietly. You lose contact with your own interests, your own friendships, and your own emotional needs. You may begin to feel resentful but unable to express it, because expressing frustration with someone who is suffering feels heartless. You may develop symptoms of your own: sleep disruption, anxiety, hypervigilance, a persistent sense of being on call. As we will discuss more fully in Chapter 8, absorbing your partner's distress over time can affect your own nervous system in measurable ways.

For your partner, the cost is less obvious but equally real. When you manage their activations, research their condition, and steer conversations away from difficulty, you are communicating something they may not consciously register but their nervous system certainly does: that they are too fragile to manage their own life. The caretaker dynamic infantilizes the survivor. It says, without words, "I do not trust you to handle this, so I will handle it for you." Over time, this erodes your partner's sense of agency, the very thing that Complex PTSD has already damaged.

Hugo saw this clearly when Lucia told him, during an honest conversation, that his constant checking in had started to feel like surveillance. "When you ask me three times if I'm okay," she said, "it makes me feel like you're waiting for me to fall apart." Hugo had been checking in because he cared. Lucia experienced it as evidence that he expected her to fail. Both readings were valid. The behavior was the same, but its impact had shifted from supportive to undermining without Hugo realizing it.

The Line Between Support and Responsibility

The distinction is simple to state and difficult to maintain. Supporting your partner's healing means being present, consistent, and willing to learn about their experience. Being responsible for their healing means taking ownership of their emotional state, their recovery progress, and their daily functioning. The first is the work of a partner. The second is the work of a clinician.

Here are some practical signals that you may be crossing the line. You find yourself managing their mood before they have asked you to. You research their condition more than they do. You feel guilty when they have a bad day, as though you could have prevented it. You cancel your own plans to accommodate their emotional state, routinely rather than occasionally. You have become the first person they call when distressed, ahead of their therapist or their friends. You avoid expressing your own needs because you do not want to add to their burden.

If three or more of those resonate, the slide has already begun. Recognizing it is not a failure. It is information, and it is the first step toward correcting the imbalance before it becomes the permanent shape of the relationship.

Encouraging Professional Support Without Issuing an Ultimatum

One of the hardest conversations in early dating with a Complex PTSD survivor is the conversation about therapy. If your partner is already in treatment, this section may be less relevant. If they are not, or if their current treatment does not seem to be addressing the patterns that are affecting your relationship, you will eventually need to raise the subject.

The instinct to say "You need to see a therapist" is understandable. The approach rarely works. For a person with Complex PTSD, being told they need professional help can land as one more piece of evidence that they are broken, that they are too much, and that the people who care about them will eventually give up. The instruction, however well-intentioned, activates the same shame and inadequacy that sit at the core of the condition.

A better approach is to frame therapy as a resource rather than a prescription, and to make it feel ordinary by discussing your own willingness to seek support. Noemi told Julian, "I've been thinking about finding a therapist for myself, because this relationship matters to me and I want to show up well. It made me wonder if you've ever thought about finding someone too." She did not present therapy as something Julian needed because he was broken. She presented it as something both of them could use, because the relationship was worth investing in.

If your partner resists, respect the resistance. You cannot force someone into treatment. You can, however, be clear about what you need. "I care about you, and I am committed to this relationship. I am also noticing that there are patterns between us that I do not think we can work through alone. I would feel better if we both had professional support." This is not an ultimatum. It is an honest statement of where you are and what you believe would help. Your partner's response will tell you a great deal about where they are and what they are ready for.

What Your Role Actually Looks Like

If you are not their therapist, what are you? You are the person who shows up consistently. You are the person who learns about Complex PTSD, as you are doing right now, so that you can understand what you are seeing without needing to fix it. You are the person who communicates your own needs honestly. You are the person who holds the relationship steady during turbulent stretches, not by absorbing all the turbulence, but by remaining present and grounded within it.

You are also the person who maintains your own life. Your friendships, your hobbies, your work, your physical health, your time alone: these are not luxuries that can be sacrificed in service of the relationship. They are the infrastructure that allows you to be a partner rather than a caretaker. When you stop attending to your own well-being, you do not become a better partner. You become a more depleted one, and depletion produces the very resentment, fatigue, and emotional flatness that will eventually make your relationship unsustainable.

Felix learned this lesson the hard way. After three months of organizing his entire schedule around Margot's emotional needs, he had a moment of clarity during a weekend when Margot was visiting her sister. He realized he had nothing to do. Not because he was lazy, but because he had let every activity, every friendship, and every personal interest atrophy in favor of being available. The empty weekend was not a relief. It was a mirror, and what it showed him was a person who had hollowed himself out in the name of being helpful. He called his oldest friend that afternoon, apologized for disappearing, and made plans to go climbing the following weekend. It was a small act, but it was the beginning of reclaiming the parts of himself that the caretaker role had quietly consumed.

This week, do one thing that is entirely your own, something that has nothing to do with your partner or your partner's healing. See a friend. Return to an activity you have neglected. Spend an evening doing something purely for your own enjoyment. Notice how it feels. If it feels selfish, notice that too, because the belief that attending to your own needs is selfish is often the first sign that the caretaker slide has already reshaped your thinking.

In a Nutshell

The caretaker slide begins with empathy and ends with depletion. It follows a predictable path: empathy leads to action, action becomes routine, routine becomes identity, and identity produces exhaustion. Recognizing the slide early is the best defense against it.

The caretaker dynamic hurts both partners. It burns out the caretaker and infantilizes the survivor, eroding the agency that Complex PTSD has already damaged.

Supporting your partner's healing means being present, consistent, and willing to learn. Being responsible for their healing means managing their emotional state, their recovery, and their daily functioning. The first is a partner's work. The second belongs to a clinician.

Encouraging professional support works best when framed as a shared investment rather than a prescription for something broken. Respect resistance, but be honest about what you need.

Your role is to show up, to maintain your own life, and to hold the relationship steady without absorbing all of its turbulence. The infrastructure of your own well-being is not a luxury. It is the thing that allows you to be a partner instead of a project manager.

Chapter 8 Your Stuff Is in the Room Too

Gabriel did not think of himself as someone with baggage. He had a stable job, good friends, and a family he described as "normal, maybe a little boring." He had never been to therapy. He had never been in an abusive relationship. When he started dating Valeria, he saw himself clearly as the steady one, the person whose job it was to provide the calm center that her history required.

It took four months and a conversation with a friend who happened to be a counselor for Gabriel to see something he had missed. His friend listened to him describe the relationship, the accommodations he was making, the careful way he managed Valeria's emotional states, the satisfaction he felt when he could prevent a difficult moment before it arrived, and then asked a question that stopped Gabriel cold: "Who taught you that love means fixing someone?"

Gabriel did not have an answer. But the question opened a door he had not known was closed. Over the following weeks, he began to notice things about himself that had nothing to do with Valeria's Complex PTSD. He noticed that he had always been the fixer in relationships. He noticed that he felt most needed, and therefore most valuable, when someone was struggling. He noticed that the moments when Valeria was doing well, when she did not need him to manage anything, produced a low hum of anxiety in his chest, as though his worth depended on her difficulty.

Gabriel was not broken. But he was not baggage-free either. And his unexamined patterns were shaping the relationship just as powerfully as Valeria's diagnosed ones.

This chapter turns the mirror toward you. It is not comfortable reading. But it may be the most important chapter in this book, because the dynamic between you and your partner is not a one-person system. Your history, your attachment patterns, your reasons for being drawn to this relationship, and your ways of coping with its challenges are all active ingredients in what the two of you are building together. Ignoring them does not make them disappear. It makes them invisible, and invisible forces are the ones that cause the most damage.

The Familiar Pull

If you have ever wondered why you feel so strongly about this particular person, so drawn to the intensity, so willing to absorb the difficulty, the answer may not be purely romantic. For many partners of Complex PTSD survivors, the relationship activates something familiar, something that feels like home, even when home was not an entirely comfortable place.

This does not mean you had a traumatic childhood. It means that most people carry patterns from their family of origin that shape who they are attracted to and how they behave in relationships. If you grew up with a parent who was emotionally unpredictable, you may find the push-pull cycle, described in Chapter 3, more tolerable than someone whose childhood was stable. The rollercoaster does not feel good, but it feels known, and known can be mistaken for right.

If you grew up in a household where your role was to manage other people's emotions, to be the peacekeeper, the good child, the one who kept things from falling apart, you may find the caretaker role, described in Chapter 7, almost irresistible. It is not that you chose to become a caretaker. It is that the role was so deeply practiced in childhood that slipping into it in adulthood requires no conscious effort at all.

Julian, whom we first met in Chapter 1, was on the other side of this equation. When he began to understand his own Complex PTSD, he also began to see how his partners had been drawn to the dynamic for their own reasons. "Noemi was attracted to my intensity," he told his therapist. "But I think she was also attracted to feeling needed. And I was attracted to her steadiness, but also to the way her steadiness let me stay in my patterns without being challenged." The relationship was not one-sided. Both of them were contributing to its shape, and both of them had work to do.

Take a few minutes to think about your own family. Who managed the emotions in your household? What role did you play? Were you the responsible one, the caretaker, the fixer, the peacemaker? And does the role you are playing in this relationship feel familiar? You are not looking for blame. You are looking for patterns, because patterns that operate outside awareness are the ones that have the most power.

Your Nervous System Is Responding Too

Chapter 2 described how your partner's nervous system reacts to perceived danger. What that chapter did not address is that your nervous system is doing its own work in response. The clinical term for this is **secondary traumatic stress**, and it describes the process by which prolonged exposure to another person's trauma responses begins to produce trauma-like symptoms in the person witnessing them (Figley, 1995).

You may not think of yourself as someone affected by trauma. But if you have been dating a Complex PTSD survivor for several months, check in with yourself honestly. Are you sleeping as well as you were before this relationship began? Do you feel more anxious than usual? Have you developed a heightened sensitivity to your partner's moods, scanning their face and voice for signs of a shift the way they scan their environment for signs of danger? Do you think about the relationship more than you think about anything else?

Paloma noticed these changes in herself gradually and then all at once. She had been dating her partner for five months when she realized that she had stopped being able to relax. Even on evenings when they were apart, she was monitoring her phone, anticipating a distressed message, bracing for the next difficult moment. Her body was in a state of low-grade activation that she had not chosen and had not noticed creeping in. When she described this to a friend, the friend said, "That sounds exactly like what you've been describing about your partner." Paloma went quiet. The parallel had not occurred to her.

Secondary traumatic stress does not mean your relationship is harmful. It means that close contact with another person's distress produces physiological effects in your own body over time, and those effects deserve attention. This is one of the strongest arguments for seeking your own therapeutic support, not because you are damaged, but because you are human, and humans absorb what they are exposed to.

The Difference Between Empathy and Enmeshment

Empathy is the ability to feel with another person, to understand their experience from the inside while maintaining your own separate perspective. Enmeshment is the loss of that separateness, the state in which your partner's feelings become your feelings, their bad day becomes your bad day, and their emotional climate becomes the weather you live in.

In early dating with a Complex PTSD survivor, the line between empathy and enmeshment can blur quickly. Marcel described the shift this way: "At first, I felt compassion when she was struggling. After a while, I started feeling the struggle as though it were mine. I could not tell where her distress ended and my distress began. When she was having a good day, I felt relief. When she was having a bad day, I felt dread. My entire emotional state was organized around hers."

If your emotional life has become a mirror of your partner's, that is enmeshment. It is not a sign of deep love. It is a sign that the separation between your internal experience and theirs has dissolved, and that dissolution will eventually produce burnout or resentment or both.

Coralie recognized enmeshment in herself when she noticed that she had started dreading her phone. Every notification produced a flash of anxiety, because the content of the message would determine her emotional state for the next several hours. A cheerful text from Oscar meant she could relax. A terse one meant her stomach would knot. And no text at all meant she would spend the evening in a fog of anticipatory dread, unable to concentrate on anything else. Her phone had become a mood-regulating device, and the mood it regulated was not hers.

The correction is not to stop caring. The correction is to rebuild the separation between your experience and theirs. This can be as simple as asking yourself, regularly, "What am I feeling right now that is mine, independent of what my partner is feeling?" Some days the answer will be clear. Other days it will not be. The practice of asking is what matters, because the question itself reinforces the distinction that enmeshment erodes.

Getting Your Own Support

There is a persistent belief, rarely stated but widely held, that the partner of a trauma survivor does not need professional help. They are the "well" one. They are the support system. They do not have a diagnosis. Seeking therapy for themselves can feel like an overreaction, like taking resources they do not deserve, or like admitting that they are failing at the job of being a good partner.

This belief is wrong, and it is dangerous. A therapist can help you identify the family-of-origin patterns that may be driving your behavior in this relationship. A therapist can help you process the secondary traumatic stress that accumulates over months of close contact with a dysregulated nervous system. A therapist can give you a space to express frustration, fear, and doubt without worrying about how your words will affect your partner. And a therapist can help you maintain the clarity you need to make good decisions about the relationship, including the decision we will address in Chapter 9.

Valeria told Gabriel, after they had been together for nearly a year, that the best thing he had ever done for their relationship was starting his own therapy. "When you stopped trying to fix me and started looking at yourself," she said, "everything between us got easier. Not because you changed who you were. Because you started seeing the whole picture instead of just my half of it."

If you have not yet considered therapy for yourself, consider it now. You do not need a crisis to justify it. You need a relationship that matters to you, a set of patterns that deserve examination, and a willingness to do the kind of honest internal work that most people avoid. That is enough.

In a Nutshell

Your history is active in this relationship. The patterns you learned in your family of origin, the roles you played, the things you were taught about love and caretaking, are shaping how you show up with your partner. Identifying those patterns is not about blame. It is about awareness.

Secondary traumatic stress is real. Prolonged exposure to your partner's distress can produce changes in your own sleep, anxiety levels, and emotional regulation. These changes deserve attention and support.

Empathy means feeling with your partner while maintaining your own separate experience. Enmeshment means losing that separateness, organizing your entire emotional life around theirs. Rebuilding the distinction is essential.

Getting your own therapist is not an overreaction. It is one of the most useful things you can do for yourself and for this relationship. You do not need a diagnosis to justify professional support. You need a willingness to look at the whole picture.

Chapter 9 The Hardest Question

Oscar sat in his car outside Eloise's apartment for forty-five minutes before driving home. He had come to pick her up for dinner. She had not responded to his text confirming the time, and her lights were off. He called once and it went to voicemail. He waited, because by now, after five months, he knew the pattern. She might be inside, frozen, unable to answer the door. She might have forgotten and gone to a friend's house. She might have decided she needed space and not told him.

He drove home, made himself dinner alone, and sat at his kitchen table with a question he had been carrying for weeks. The question was simple and enormous: Should I stay?

He loved Eloise. He understood her. He had read about Complex PTSD, had adjusted his behavior, had learned to regulate his own responses during difficult moments. He had done everything this book describes. And he was still, on a Tuesday evening in January, eating pasta by himself in a dark kitchen while the woman he loved was unreachable for reasons he would never fully know.

Oscar's question is the one that every partner of a Complex PTSD survivor eventually faces. It is also the one that almost no book, no blog post, and no well-meaning friend has the courage to answer honestly. The advice is always the same: be patient, be understanding, educate yourself, try harder. Nobody says the other thing, the thing that also needs to be said: sometimes, despite your best efforts and your deepest feelings, the answer is that this relationship is not right for you. And sometimes, with equal honesty, the answer is that it is.

This chapter will not make the decision for you. But it will give you a framework for making it well, one based on your values and the evidence in front of you, rather than on guilt, exhaustion, or the sunk cost of months already invested.

Hard Is Not the Same as Harmful

Every relationship involves difficulty. The question is never "Is this hard?" The question is "Is this the kind of hard that leads somewhere?" All worthwhile relationships ask their participants to stretch, to accommodate, to learn new skills, and to tolerate discomfort. A relationship with a Complex PTSD survivor asks more of these things, more often, and with higher emotional stakes. That is hard, but it is not, by itself, harmful.

Harmful is different. Harmful is a steady erosion of your sense of self. Harmful is a pattern in which your needs are consistently dismissed, your feelings are routinely invalidated, and your attempts at connection are met with contempt rather than difficulty. Harmful is the feeling that you are shrinking, that you are less yourself than you were six months ago, that the person you are becoming inside this relationship is someone you would not recognize from the outside.

Sebastian asked himself this question after a particularly difficult stretch with his partner. He was tired. He was frustrated. He had given more than he thought he had to give. But when he sat with the question honestly, he realized that he was still himself. He was still seeing friends. He was still doing work he cared about. He was still able to laugh, to think clearly, and to feel his own feelings independently of his partner's emotional state. He was stretched. He was not diminished. And the difference between those two things was, for Sebastian, the answer.

If you are stretched but still yourself, the relationship may be hard in a way that is worth enduring. If you are diminished, if you are losing access to your own identity, your own needs, and your own voice, the difficulty has crossed into a different territory.

Signs That Point Toward Staying

Not all relationships with Complex PTSD survivors are the same, and the presence of the condition is not, by itself, a reason to stay or leave. What matters is what both of you are doing with it. Here are the signs that suggest this relationship has a genuine foundation for growth.

Your partner acknowledges their Complex PTSD and its effects. They may not use that exact term. But they recognize that their reactions are sometimes disproportionate, that their patterns affect you, and that the difficulty is not something you caused. This acknowledgment does not need to be eloquent. It just needs to be real.

Your partner is pursuing treatment or is open to it. They may already be in therapy. They may be researching options. They may have told you, honestly, that they are not ready yet but that they understand why it matters. The key signal is movement, not perfection.

Repair happens after rupture. This is one of the most reliable indicators of a healthy relationship, with or without Complex PTSD. When something goes wrong, do both of you find your way back? Does your partner take responsibility for their part, even if it takes time? As we discussed in Chapter 3, the push-pull cycle is not the problem. The inability to repair after the cycle is.

Your needs are received, even imperfectly. When you express what you need, does your partner hear you? They do not need to meet every need immediately. They need to receive them without dismissal, and to make effort over time. If your needs are consistently met with defensiveness or indifference, that is a different signal.

You can name your own feelings in this relationship. If you feel able to say "I'm frustrated" or "I need something different tonight" without fear of an explosion or a days-long withdrawal, the relational climate is healthy enough to hold honest communication.

Signs That Have Nothing to Do with Complex PTSD

This section must be direct. Complex PTSD can explain certain behaviors: the withdrawal, the emotional intensity, the difficulty with closeness. It cannot and should not explain everything. There are behaviors that are harmful regardless of their origin, and labeling them as trauma responses does not make them acceptable.

Persistent cruelty. If your partner is consistently cruel, if they use language designed to wound, if they mock your vulnerabilities or undermine your confidence, that is not a trauma response. That is how they treat you, and no amount of clinical understanding will make it bearable over time.

Refusal to take any responsibility. A person with Complex PTSD may struggle with accountability, especially during activated states. But if your partner consistently attributes every problem to you, refuses to acknowledge any part they play in the relationship's difficulties, and responds to honest feedback with deflection or attack, the pattern is larger than Complex PTSD.

Using the diagnosis as a blanket excuse. "I have Complex PTSD" is an explanation, not a permission slip. If your partner uses it to shut down every conversation about their behavior, to avoid making any changes, or to position you as heartless for having needs, the diagnosis has become a tool rather than a truth.

Any form of physical aggression or intimidation. This requires no qualification. There is no trauma history that justifies physical violence or the threat of it. If your physical safety is at risk, the only appropriate response is to remove yourself from the situation and seek help.

Clara, who had invested months in understanding and accommodating her partner's patterns, eventually confronted a difficult truth: some of the behaviors she had been attributing to Complex PTSD were simply how her partner chose to behave. The withdrawal was a trauma response. The contemptuous comments about her intelligence were not. Separating the two took time, the help of her own therapist, and a willingness to see what she had not wanted to see. But making that separation was the thing that finally allowed her to make a clear decision.

The Sunk Cost Trap

Three months of effort does not obligate you to a lifetime of suffering. Six months of effort does not either. The time you have already invested in this relationship is not a reason to continue investing if the return is consistently negative.

Ines told her therapist, "I keep thinking about all the work I've done, all the books I've read, all the patience I've shown. If I leave now, doesn't that mean it was all for nothing?" Her therapist responded, "Everything you've learned applies to the rest of your life. None of it disappears if this relationship ends.

The only thing that would be wasted is the time you spend from this point forward in a relationship that is causing you more harm than growth."

This is not permission to leave at the first sign of difficulty. This is permission to evaluate the relationship as it is now, not as it was three months ago, not as you hope it will be three months from now, but as it actually is today. If the answer to "Is this relationship making me a smaller version of myself?" is yes, then the length of time you have spent in it is irrelevant. The decision to leave is about the future, not the past.

Leaving with Compassion and Staying with Intention

If you decide to leave, you can do so with honesty and kindness. A conversation that sounds like this: "I care about you, and I have tried to show up for this relationship in every way I know how. I am not leaving because of your past or because you are too much. I am leaving because I am not able to be the partner you need while also being the person I need to be." This is not a rejection of your partner. It is an acknowledgment that love, on its own, is not always enough, and that recognizing that is an act of honesty, not cruelty.

If you decide to stay, do so with intention rather than default. A decision to stay should sound like this, at least in your own mind: "I am choosing this relationship because I see growth, because I believe in what we are building, and because the difficulty is the kind that leads somewhere. I am not staying because I feel guilty, because I am afraid to leave, or because I do not believe I deserve something easier."

Lucia made her decision to stay with Hugo after sitting with the question for two full weeks. She wrote in her journal every evening. She talked to her therapist. She talked to her closest friend. And at the end of two weeks, she realized that the answer was clear. Hugo was doing the work. She was doing the work. The hard moments were getting shorter. The repairs were getting faster. And on the good days, which were becoming more frequent than the hard ones, she felt something she had never felt in a relationship before: safe enough to be herself. That was worth staying for.

In a Nutshell

The question of staying or leaving is the hardest one in this book, and it deserves an honest answer. Hard is not the same as harmful. Stretch is not the same as diminishment. The difference between the two is the clearest guide you have.

Signs that this relationship is worth the effort include your partner's acknowledgment of their condition, pursuit of treatment, willingness to repair after rupture, and ability to receive your needs.

Signs that the problem goes beyond Complex PTSD include persistent cruelty, total refusal of responsibility, using the diagnosis as a blanket excuse, and any form of physical threat or violence.

The time you have already invested does not obligate you to keep investing. Evaluate the relationship as it is today, not as it was or as you hope it might become.

If you leave, do so with honesty and kindness. If you stay, do so with intention and clarity. Both decisions deserve the same quality of thought.

Chapter 10 Building Something Real

Hugo and Lucia celebrated their first anniversary on a Tuesday, which Lucia insisted was better than a weekend because Tuesdays had always been their best day. They ate at the same restaurant where they had their second date. Hugo ordered the same wine. Lucia ordered something different, because, she said, she was a different person now.

She was not being dramatic. Over the course of twelve months, the patterns that had defined their early relationship had not disappeared, but they had changed. The freeze responses were less frequent and shorter in duration. The withdrawals were still there, but Lucia had learned to say, before she pulled away, "I need some time. I'll be back tomorrow." The silences that had once lasted days now lasted hours. And when they reconnected, the repair was faster, more honest, and less laden with shame.

Hugo had changed too, in ways he had not expected. He was less reactive to Lucia's shifts. He had learned, through his own therapy and through the months of practice, to recognize when her nervous system was speaking and to respond to the nervous system rather than to the surface behavior. He had also learned something about himself: that his need to fix things was its own kind of pattern, and that sitting still beside someone in pain, without doing anything about it, was one of the hardest and most loving skills he had ever developed.

Their relationship was not easy. It was not effortless. It was not the kind of love story that looks good on a greeting card. But it was real, and it was growing, and both of them knew, with a certainty that had been tested many times, that what they were building was worth the work it required.

This final chapter is about what becomes possible when both partners show up, not perfectly, but consistently. It is not a promise that everything will be fine. It is a description of what progress actually looks like in a relationship where Complex PTSD is present, and a practical guide for building the kind of foundation that can hold both partners for the long term.

What Getting Better Actually Looks Like

If you are waiting for a day when Complex PTSD is gone, when your partner is fully healed and your relationship is free of the patterns described in this book, you will be waiting for something that may never arrive. Complex PTSD is a condition that can be managed, reduced in its intensity, and significantly improved with sustained treatment. It is not, in most cases, something that disappears entirely.

This is not a discouraging statement. It is a realistic one, and realism is a better foundation for commitment than fantasy. What getting better actually looks like is not the absence of difficulty. It is a change in the difficulty's shape.

Mateo noticed this shift around month eight with Ines. The push-pull cycle, which had once been a source of genuine crisis, had become something more like a weather pattern. He could see it coming. He knew approximately how long it would last. He had learned not to take it personally, and Ines had learned to communicate, imperfectly but consistently, when she was entering a withdrawal phase. The storm still happened, but it was no longer a hurricane. It was a passing rain. They had umbrellas, and they knew where to stand.

Recovery from Complex PTSD is not linear. Your partner will have good weeks and hard weeks, good months and difficult ones. Progress shows up not as a steady upward line, but as a pattern in which the hard moments become less intense, shorter in duration, and more quickly repaired. Track these changes. They are easy to miss when you are inside the relationship, and they are the most reliable measure of growth.

Earned Secure Attachment Is Real

The clinical literature contains a concept that may be the most hopeful idea in this entire book. It is called **earned secure attachment**, and it describes the process by which a person who did not develop secure attachment in childhood can build it in adulthood through consistent, safe relational experiences (Roisman et al., 2002).

Your partner's attachment system was shaped by early relationships that were unsafe. But attachment systems are not fixed. The brain is capable of forming new relational templates throughout life, a process neuroscientists call neuroplasticity. When your partner experiences, over and over again, that you are reliable, that you do not punish them for pulling away, that you return after conflict, and that your affection is not conditional on their performance, their nervous system begins to update its predictions. Slowly, at its own pace, the system starts to believe that closeness might not be dangerous after all.

This does not happen in weeks or months. It happens over years of consistent experience. And it does not happen because of any single grand gesture. It happens because of the accumulation of small, reliable moments: the text that arrives when you said it would, the calm response to a difficult evening, the morning after a rupture when you are still there, still warm, still present.

Zoe told Elio, on their first anniversary, that she had noticed something she could not explain. "I used to feel afraid every time you left my apartment," she said, "like you might not come back. I still feel it sometimes. But now there's another feeling underneath it, a feeling that says you probably will. I've never had that before." That second feeling, the one underneath the fear, is the beginning of earned secure attachment. It does not replace the fear. It sits alongside it, and over time, it grows larger.

Co-Creating a Relationship Culture

Every relationship develops its own culture: the unspoken rules, the shared language, the rituals, and the norms that define how the two people operate together. In a relationship where Complex PTSD is present, co-creating this culture intentionally, rather than letting it form around the condition, is one of the most important things you can do.

This means developing shared language for difficult moments. Valeria and Gabriel created a shorthand: when Valeria said "the weather is changing," Gabriel knew she was entering a difficult emotional state and needed space without a conversation about why. When Gabriel said "I need to put my own mask on," Valeria knew he was reaching the edge of his capacity and needed time for himself. These phrases were not clinical. They were theirs, and they worked because both partners had agreed on their meaning in advance.

This means establishing repair rituals. Felix and Margot, who had struggled with ruptures in their early months, developed a practice of "the next morning conversation." The rule was simple: after a difficult evening, neither partner would try to process it that night. The next morning, over coffee, one of them would say, "Last night was hard. Are you okay?" The question was an invitation, not a demand. Sometimes it led to a conversation. Sometimes the answer was simply "Yeah, I'm okay," and they moved on. The ritual was not about the content. It was about the reliability of the reconnection.

This means building rituals that have nothing to do with Complex PTSD. The condition will take up space in your relationship. It should not take up all the space. Mateo and Ines made a rule: one evening per week was declared a no-processing zone. No conversations about feelings, patterns, or activation states. Just dinner, a walk, a film, a board game, ordinary couple activities that reminded both of them that their relationship was larger than its most challenging dimension.

The Long View

Research on relationships where one partner has experienced significant trauma suggests that outcomes vary enormously depending on several factors: the quality of professional treatment, the consistency of the non-traumatized partner's support, the couple's ability to communicate about the impact of trauma on the relationship, and the willingness of both partners to grow (Johnson, 2008). The prognosis is not determined by the severity of the trauma. It is determined by what both people do with it.

Here is what the research, and the experience of countless couples, suggests is possible. It is possible for your partner's nervous system to recalibrate over time in the context of a safe relationship. It is possible for the push-pull cycle to become less extreme. It is possible for emotional flashbacks to become shorter and less disorienting. It is possible for trust, real trust, to grow in soil that was once poisoned. It is possible for physical intimacy to become a source of connection rather than activation. And it is possible for both of you, not just your partner, to emerge from this period of your lives with a deeper understanding of yourselves than you had before.

It is also possible that, despite your best efforts, the relationship will not work out. That possibility does not negate the effort. As we discussed in Chapter 9, the skills you develop in this relationship travel with you. The patience, the emotional literacy, the ability to hold space for complexity without drowning in it: these are not wasted if the relationship ends. They are yours permanently.

A Final, Honest Note

This relationship will ask more of you than a relationship with someone who does not carry Complex PTSD. That is simply true. It is not noble. It is not pathological. It is not a sign of extraordinary love or extraordinary foolishness. It is the reality of choosing to build something with a person whose nervous system was shaped by experiences that left deep marks.

The question has never been "Will this be hard?" The question has always been "Is what we are building worth what it costs us both?" If the answer is yes, then what you have is not just a relationship. It is something rarer: a partnership that has been tested, examined, and chosen with open eyes.

Your partner did not choose their history. You did not choose to fall in love with someone who carries it. But you can choose, both of you, what you do from here. And that choice, made again and again across the hundreds of ordinary days that make up a life together, is the most powerful thing either of you will ever do.

Before you close this book, sit down together if you can. Talk about what kind of relationship you want to build. Not the relationship you have today, but the one you are working toward. Write it down if that helps. Discuss what each of you needs to feel safe, what each of you needs to feel valued, and what you will do the next time things get hard, because they will get hard again. This is not a weakness in your relationship. This is the work of two people who understand that love, on its own, is not enough, and who have decided to add to it the things that are: patience, honesty, repair, and the willingness to keep choosing each other in the full light of what that choice requires.

In a Nutshell

Progress in Complex PTSD recovery is not linear. It shows up as a change in the shape of difficulty: less intense, shorter in duration, more quickly repaired. Track these changes, because they are easy to miss from the inside.

Earned secure attachment is clinically documented and achievable. Your partner's nervous system can form new relational templates through years of consistent, safe experience. This process is slow, but it is real.

Co-creating a relationship culture means developing shared language for difficult moments, establishing repair rituals, and building experiences that have nothing to do with Complex PTSD. The condition should occupy space in your relationship. It should not occupy all the space.

This relationship will ask more of you. That is not noble or pathological. It is true. The question is not about the difficulty. The question is about what you are building together, and your answer to that question is something only the two of you can provide.

References

- Ainsworth, M. D. S., Blehar, M. C., Waters, E., & Wall, S. (1978). *Patterns of attachment: A psychological study of the strange situation.* Lawrence Erlbaum Associates.

- Braman, L. (2021). *How to tell a friend or partner about your past trauma.* Lindsay Braman Illustration and Education.

- Cloitre, M., Garvert, D. W., Brewin, C. R., Bryant, R. A., & Maercker, A. (2013). Evidence for proposed ICD-11 PTSD and complex PTSD: A latent profile analysis. *European Journal of Psychotraumatology, 4*(1), Article 20706.

- Figley, C. R. (1995). Compassion fatigue as secondary traumatic stress disorder: An overview. In C. R. Figley (Ed.), *Compassion fatigue: Coping with secondary traumatic stress disorder in those who treat the traumatized* (pp. 1–20). Brunner/Mazel.

- Gottman, J. M., & Silver, N. (1999). *The seven principles for making marriage work.* Crown Publishers.

- Herman, J. L. (1992). Complex PTSD: A syndrome in survivors of prolonged and repeated trauma. *Journal of Traumatic Stress, 5*(3), 377–391.

- Johnson, S. M. (2008). *Hold me tight: Seven conversations for a lifetime of love.* Little, Brown and Company.

- Main, M., & Hesse, E. (1990). Parents' unresolved traumatic experiences are related to infant disorganized attachment status: Is frightened and/or frightening parental behavior the linking mechanism? In M. T. Greenberg, D. Cicchetti, & E. M. Cummings (Eds.), *Attachment in the preschool years: Theory, research, and intervention* (pp. 161–182). University of Chicago Press.

- Porges, S. W. (2011). *The polyvagal theory: Neurophysiological foundations of emotions, attachment, communication, and self-regulation.* W. W. Norton.

- Roisman, G. I., Padrón, E., Sroufe, L. A., & Egeland, B. (2002). Earned-secure attachment status in retrospect and prospect. *Child Development, 73*(4), 1204–1219.

- Siegel, D. J. (2012). *The developing mind: How relationships and the brain interact to shape who we are* (2nd ed.). Guilford Press.

- van der Kolk, B. A. (2014). *The body keeps the score: Brain, mind, and body in the healing of trauma.* Viking.

- Walker, P. (2013). *Complex PTSD: From surviving to thriving: A guide and map for recovering from childhood trauma.* Azure Coyote.

- World Health Organization. (2019). *International classification of diseases 11th revision (ICD-11).*